FIRE IN YOUR HEART

FIRE IN YOUR HEART

by

SAMMY TIPPIT

MOODY PRESS
CHICAGO

Library of Congress Cataloging in Publication Data

Tippit, Sammy.
  Fire in your heart.

  1. Tippit, Sammy.   2. Evangelists —Biography.
3. Revivals —Europe —Church history.   I. Title.
BV3785.T553A3   1987   274.7'0828   86-31229
ISBN 0-8024-2625-5

9 10 8

Printed in the United States of America

To my wife, Tex, and our children, Dave and Renée, who have stood with me as I have ministered in the East.

To the late Ken Leeburg, who taught me to climb a hill called "Difficulty."

To the believers in Eastern Europe, who have been used of God to start a fire in my heart. This is their story.

CONTENTS

FOREWORD

We live in curious times. Never has there been so much activity done in the name of the Lord, but rarely have people's hearts been more cold toward the things of the Lord. In some Christian circles, concern with self-esteem has overshadowed the biblical emphasis on deep repentance and heartfelt confession of sin. Churches have grown fat and indolent. Form and function have replaced substance and truth. The hearts of God's people need to again be set aflame from on high.

Sammy Tippit has witnessed the flames of genuine revival in an unlikely place—Eastern Europe. His ministry there has given him a new understanding of the promise that "with God all things are possible" (Matthew 19:26). But it has also opened his eyes anew to the fact that following Christ means taking up a cross.

Westerners may be surprised to hear of revival behind the Iron Curtain—or of North Americans like Sammy who are active in ministry among Christians there. But God is doing marvelous things to build His church in Eastern Europe. In many ways it is healthier, more vibrant, and more aggressive than the church in the free world.

His ministry behind the Iron Curtain uniquely equips Sammy to write on the subject of fire in the heart. In communist Europe he has been exposed to a brand of Christianity so earnest that its people are known as "repenters." He has ministered to Christians whose faith literally costs them everything. He has worked hand in hand with men like Josif Ton, whom God raised up out of Romania to challenge both the arrogant atheism of the communist states and the creeping lethargy of the church.

My eyes were first opened to God's marvelous work behind the Iron Curtain when I met Josif Ton several years ago. He told me of the church he pastored, where more than a thousand would stand outside in the cold and snow, straining to hear God's Word, because they couldn't get into the little church building. He lamented the apathy of Western Christians and gently told me he thought a little persecution would be good for the church in America. He is right. Nothing fans the flame of the heart like winds of adversity.

Those of us who minister in North American must resist two dangerous inclinations. First, we must not think that the hype and ballyhoo we see in so much of contemporary Christianity equals true revival. It has nothing to do with real fire from heaven. Sammy Tippit calls it "wildfire." And it is especially dangerous wildfire. It bears a resemblance to the real thing, but instead of providing light and heat, it brings only destruction and ashes.

Second, we must not fall into indifference, thinking that serving the Lord is meant to be a comfortable experience. Real faith cannot sit passively on the sidelines, living a life of ease. Fruitless faith is dead faith (James 2:17). And faith that costs nothing is worth nothing.

Fire in Your Heart is an urgent call for Christians to return to a wholehearted faith. It is a reminder to all of us that if there is to be a great awakening in our time, we are the ones who must wake up.

JOHN MACARTHUR, JR.

PREFACE

For centuries the torch of the gospel of Jesus Christ has been brought from Western civilization to the rest of the world. However, now an entirely different situation has developed. We hear of spiritual awakening in Africa and South America, in Korea, and parts of Eastern Europe. However, the West as a whole remains unaffected.

Perhaps the church has been wounded from the higher critics and rationalists. We seem to be struggling, groping in the dark. Occasional fires can be seen, but upon closer examination, many appear to be wildfire rather than heavenly fire. It is not the fire of Luther, Wesley, Moody, Whitefield, or the great awakeners of past years.

We have the technology, the knowledge, and the manpower, but not the *fire*, the fire from God that burns in the hearts of His people for a lost and dying world. It is this fire that burns away the superficial and purifies that work which God has begun in the hearts of men.

Fire in Your Heart is a message based on three primary sources: the Bible, history, and the lives of those presently experiencing awakening. In twelve years of ministry in Eastern Europe, I have found true revival in many parts of Romania, the Soviet Union, and some parts of the German Democratic Republic (East Germany). *Fire in Your Heart* speaks of a fire of simplicity, purity, boldness, and love.

I have personally been touched by this fire, and now a

flame burns within my heart. My desire is that this fire will spread throughout the Western world. We have sophisticated technology, but they have simple theology. We have learned Hollywood-style evangelism, but they have practiced Spirit-anointed evangelism. Our heroes are athletes. Theirs are martyrs. My prayer is that this fire from the East will become fire in your heart.

1
VISION FOR AWAKENING

Let God send the fire of His Spirit here, and the minister will be more and more lost in his Master. You will come to think less of the speaker and more of the truth spoken. . . .

Let God but send down the fire, and the biggest sinners in the neighborhood will be converted; those who live in the dens of infamy will be changed; the drunkard will forsake his cups, the swearer will repent of his blasphemy, the debauched will leave their lusts—

Dry bones be raised and clothed afresh,
And hearts of stone be turned to flesh.[1]
　　　　　　　—Charles H. Spurgeon

In East Berlin's Alexanderplatz, well over 100,000 communist young people gathered for the Communist Youth World Festival. They represented every nation in the world. Everywhere I looked there was nothing but young people, policemen, and soldiers. It was the summer of 1973.

The atmosphere was electric. The sun was shining. The air was cool. The borders were jammed, and the city

1. Arnold Dallimore, *Spurgeon* (Chicago. Moody, 1984), p. 42.

was geared up for the Festival. This was to be one of the most important days of my life.

It all began a year earlier when I met Pastor Bush. I had been preaching evangelistic campaigns in West Berlin. Because I wanted to meet some believers from Eastern Europe, a friend brought me with him on a visit to East Berlin. There he introduced me to the elderly pastor. During the Hitler regime, he had been arrested and imprisoned for refusing to instruct his congregation to bow to the Fuhrer. When World War II ended, he was left in East Berlin. There he circulated a letter to his Lutheran pastor colleagues, begging them not to sign a document calling Communism "the Savior of the world." As a result he was not allowed to pastor. But that did not keep him from attempting to reach the East German people with the gospel.

Pastor Bush was a man of deep prayer. He had a burden for the youth of his country. He pointed his finger at me. "Young man," he said, "next summer, young people will be gathered in East Berlin from every nation in the world. They will be trained to evangelize the world for atheism and Communism. I want you to pray about coming to that meeting and preaching the gospel."

I was shocked. "They would never let me in to preach. It's impossible!"

Pastor Bush responded with a twinkle. "Don't ever say impossible. 'With men this is impossible; but with God all things are possible!' " (Matthew 19:26).

Those words haunted me when I returned to the United States. I told two American friends about my encounter with Pastor Bush and his challenge for me to go to the Communist Youth Festival in East Berlin. Fred Bishop, Fred Starkweather, and I prayed and stepped out in faith. The impossible became possible. God did open the doors for us to be in the middle of the Communist Youth World Festival.

As we mingled with these young people, a multitude of questions raced through my mind. How would we be able to open conversations about Jesus with these young people? If we did have opportunities to speak of Christ, how would they respond to us? They had been skillfully trained in atheist teaching.

We were soon to discover that God's power is greater than the power of the atheist teachers, motivators, and philosophers of Eastern Europe.

As the three of us talked, our conversation began to draw a crowd. It was considered important at the Fest to get the autograph of a foreigner, and I guess everyone within earshot could tell easily that my German was heavily influenced by my Southern American heritage. The crowd gathered in the hope of getting the autograph of someone from the States. The young people all wore scarves on which they collected the autographs of kids from various countries.

As the kids asked us to sign their kerchiefs, the Lord gave me an idea. I pulled my two companions close and told Fred Bishop to write in German, "God loves you and has a wonderful plan for your life," before signing his name. Fred Starkweather could write, "Man's sin has separated him from this plan," and then sign his name. And before signing my name, I would write that Jesus is the only way to bridge the gap left by sin, along with a note explaining how to receive Him.

We would explain the plan of salvation to those who were curious about what we had written. We must have signed more than two hundred scarves that night alone. I felt the presence of God with us, and I also felt a special anointing of the Holy Spirit. Sensing His power at work, I began to preach. To my amazement the Communists asked many questions, and I was able to show them clearly the way to Christ.

Within the next week, 200 of these hardcore communist youth committed themselves to follow Jesus Christ. The last night of the Fest, these new believers marched through Alexanderplatz playing their guitars and singing about Jesus.

The Communists sent a thousand young people to break up the march. They ended up behind us, and we appeared to be 1,200 young people. People began to run throughout Alexanderplatz shouting, "What are we going to do? The Jesus People are coming!" Eventually we were trapped in a corner, and thousands of delegates came running to see what was taking place.

I began to pray, and as I did God clearly spoke to my heart. "You'll never again get the chance to preach to this many lost people in your life. This may be the greatest opportunity you'll ever have to tell communist youth about Me. Stand up and preach about Jesus."

"Lord," I cried, "Your strength and Your power will have to be with me. I can't do it on my own."

After calling for silence, I began to give my testimony as quickly as possible. About 2,000 communist youth burst forward, nearly trampling the 200 Christians and pushing in toward me. They were waving their fists in my face and threatening. The whole place was in an uproar as the crowd surged forward. For a moment, I thought I had preached my last sermon.

We then attempted to break our way through the crowd. As the Communists swung at me, I was overwhelmed with the joy of the Lord. God's Word leaped within my heart, "Blessed are [you] when men shall revile you" (Matthew 5:11).

I had learned the most fundamental principle of spiritual awakening: "With men it is impossible, but with God all things are possible." The old German pastor had been correct. The glory of God always shines brighter when the night is the darkest.

It is the darkness that forces men to seek the brightness of God's glory. In a museum at Checkpoint Charlie, the border crossing from West to East Berlin, there is a picture of a Lutheran pastor in East Germany who poured gasoline over his entire body and burned himself alive. He was protesting the pressure his government had placed on youth to follow atheism and Communism. Certainly the night had become dark in East Germany.

But there was a ray of hope. There were two laymen in the country who believed that God is, and "He is a rewarder of them that diligently seek Him" (Hebrews 11:6).

These men could not forget their heritage. They prayed for the young people of East Germany and asked God to send His light into their hearts. Spiritual darkness had covered that part of Germany 400 years earlier, during a period known to historians as the end of the Dark Ages. The church had become corrupt and was without power.

During that time there lived a man named Johann Tetzel. A seller of indulgences and certificates of salvation, he would travel from city to city swindling people out of their money. From a red cross placed in front of an altar, he suspended what represented the arms of the pope.

"This cross," he would say, "has as much efficacy as the very cross of Jesus Christ. Come, and I will give you letters, all properly sealed, by which even the sins that you *intend* to commit may be pardoned.

"I would not change my privileges for those of St. Peter in heaven, for I have saved more souls by my indulgences than the apostle by his sermons.

"There is no sin so great that an indulgence cannot remit . . . only let him pay well and all will be forgiven him.

"But more than this," said he, "indulgences avail not only for the living but for the dead.

"Priest! Noble! Merchant! Wife! Youth! Maiden! Do you not hear your parents and your friends who are dead and who cry from the bottom of the abyss saying, 'We are suffering horrible torments! A trifling alm would deliver us. You can give it, and you will not!'

"At the very instant," continued Tetzel, "that the money rattles at the bottom of this chest, the soul escapes from purgatory and flies liberated to heaven."[2]

In the midst of religious corruption and darkness, the glory of God broke into the heart of a young man by the name of Martin Luther. In an Augustinian monastery he read the Scriptures for the first time. *"Der Gerechte wird aus Glauben leben"* (The just shall live by faith) began to burn in his heart. Imagine Luther's joy and hope as he understood the fullness of what he read. His eyes had seen the King, a Savior who gives His love and salvation to all who simply receive it by faith.

As the fire of faith was lit in the heart of Martin Luther, the light of God's glory began to spread throughout Europe. Western civilization would never be the same.

Today it seems that darkness once again is the order of the day. Secular humanism is the rationale of this generation, while we seem to be controlled by fear. Terrorism continues to grow worldwide. Moral decay is evidenced by an outbreak of gross, sexually transmitted diseases. The problem seems equally great within the church. Many cry with despair, "Our generation is one of fear and darkness. There is no hope!"

I must respond that it's not so! I've been to one of the darkest places on earth, and I've seen the glory! At the Communist Youth World Festival I saw the glory of God. And I've seen it again even more recently.

One of the most difficult places on the earth for a Christian to live today is the nation of Romania. Christians are continually harassed there. Many lose educational and

2. J.H. Merle D'Aubigne, *The Life and Times of Martin Luther* (Chicago: Moody, 1978), pp. 92–93.

job opportunities because of their faith, and some are imprisoned. But I have seen the glory of God in Romania. I've seen the glory of God in parts of the Soviet Union and Poland as well.

My faith has been renewed, and I believe that God wants to send a great awakening in the midst of the darkness of the Western world. Spiritual awakening is simply a fresh view of Jesus. When we see Him, there is only one thing we can do. We fall at His feet in sweet surrender to love and worship Him. It is that love that spurs us to become the salt and light of the world.

There is a question that plagues me, however. With all of our freedom and heritage in the West, why don't we have revival? Everywhere I go I ask that question. The best answer came to me in Romania.

There was a pastor in Bothell, Washington, Dr. Sam Friend, with whom I had become very close. I had preached in his church several times. Dr. Friend visited Romania and met Josif Ton. Josif asked Pastor Friend to send a music group and a young pastor to preach evangelistic meetings throughout Romania. At the time I was pastor of the Hahn Baptist Church in Hahn, Germany.

I had heard of the revival in Romania, but it was through other believers in Eastern Europe that I learned how desperate the situation really was. They told me of long lines for food and gas and of power shortages in the winter. But mostly they spoke of the severe oppression of the believers by the Romanian government. Soon after accepting Josif's invitation to preach, I experienced first-hand the severity of Romanian life.

In June 1980, I boarded a Volkswagen van with five musicians and all of their sound equipment and luggage and left Hahn Baptist Church for Romania. At the Romanian border, we encountered our first difficulty. We were detained seven hours. At one point the border guards and customs people told me that we couldn't enter the country because we had so much sound equipment. We negotiated with them and left a $2,000 deposit. That was to insure that we would not sell the equipment on the black market. They searched everything in the van, finding that each of us had a personal Bible. As those were confiscated, one of the girls in the music group began to cry. "Sammy, you can't let them take my Bible."

I was puzzled. "They have machine guns. I don't think we have any choice."

But that didn't seem to comfort her. So I said, "Let's pray about it." Immediately before allowing us to cross into Romania, they gave us back our Bibles.

After spending a few days in Romania, I thought that George Orwell had visited that country before writing *1984*. One pastor told us in a restaurant to be careful with our conversation. He said that secret police were nearby. I asked him how he knew that they were secret police.

I was amazed at his response. "I've been interrogated by those men every week for six months."

Many times at the conclusion of the worship services, crowds would gather around me to ask questions and learn more about Jesus. Occasionally, the crowds would instantly disperse as someone would whisper, "Secret police." Persecution is much greater in Romania than in other Eastern bloc nations.

Yet, in the midst of the hardship stands one of the most precious groups I have ever met. The church is alive and growing. In every city where I ministered, there was never room in the church for all the people. Every seat, every inch of standing room was taken. Crowds gathered around the windows. The doors were opened, and the masses listened from outside, many times by loud speakers.

The music group would sing for an hour, and I would preach for an hour. Then we were mobbed by people wanting to hear more.

Everywhere I went, I kept hearing about Josif Ton.

He was being mightily used of God to spread the revival, especially among university students. We concluded our two weeks of preaching in his large church in Oradea. I was awed by his spirituality and scholarly approach to the Scriptures. Hundreds of key intellectuals were coming to hear him lecture every week. It was no surprise that the government forced Josif to leave Romania just a few months after we returned to Germany.

Josif continues to minister to Romania today through broadcasts and literature as president of the Romanian Missionary Society in the United States.

He says that "Eastern Europe is a post-Marxist society, while Western Europe and the United States are perhaps pre-Marxist.

"The Communists promised a utopia to Eastern Europe forty years ago. But the people are under even worse conditions now. Communism has been a failure. The new man has not emerged as promised by Marx. The people of Romania have learned what not to believe in. Now they need to know what to believe in. They are hungry for the truth."

I was reminded of the words of Jesus, "Blessed are they which do hunger and thirst after righteousness: for they shall be filled" (Matthew 5:6).

"But, Sammy," he continued, "the Western world is flirting with the underlying philosophy of Communism: secular humanism. Many nations of the Western world are like the prodigal son. Their hearts have turned away from the loving Father. They are experimenting with communist philosophy. They have not realized yet what the people of Eastern Europe have learned. No government or human philosophy can create the 'new man.' "

Herein lies the key to revival in the Western world. Revival can be defined by one word: Jesus. He is the only way to create the new man. He is the truth and the underlying philosophy for a society to function as it should. But most of all, He is life!

Somehow our view of Jesus has been clouded. In our attempt to make sure we are comfortable and free from pain, we have lost the centrality of the cross of Christ in Christianity. Christianity without the cross is not Christianity at all.

Everything in the life of Jesus pointed to the cross. The cross was ugly and painful. It was the symbol of death. On the cross Jesus paid the price to make the way for us to come to God. He gave us the contrasting picture of the love of the Father and the sinfulness of man. On the cross Jesus gave up His life that we might have life eternal.

But He says to all who would follow Him, "If any man will come after me, let him deny himself, *take up his cross daily*, and follow me" (Luke 9:23; emphasis added).

In order to follow Him, we must take up our cross. We shall never see the glory of His resurrection power until we enter into the experience of the cross. And that costs. It costs everything.

Roy Hession experienced revival in East Africa. Shortly after being touched by that revival, he was asked by a friend, "What is your vision?"

He responded that he had three visions: for evangelism, Scripture distribution, and revival.

The wise friend said, "Brother, you have not really seen the way yet. . . . How terrible! There is only one vision, and that is the Jesus you have been experiencing in the revival. He includes everything!"[3]

When He is everything, then we have all we need.

Later, when a friend returned to England from the African revival, he told Hession, "I find the Christians in England have the queerist idea of what revival is. They think

---

3. Roy Hession, *When I Saw Him* (Fort Washington, Pa.: Christian Literature Crusade, 1975), p. 85.

it is the top blowing off, when in reality it is the bottom falling out!"[4]

Jesus is the King. In His manifesto He described the inhabitants of His kingdom. Those who listened must have been shocked as they heard the King's words (Matthew 5:3-10):

> Blessed are the poor in spirit. . . .
> Blessed are they that mourn. . . .
> Blessed are the meek. . . .
> Blessed are those [who] hunger and thirst after righteousness. . . .
> Blessed are the merciful. . . .
> Blessed are the pure in heart. . . .
> Blessed are the peacemakers. . . .
> Blessed are those who are persecuted for righteousness sake. . . .

That is a description of those who have had the bottom fall out. Jesus came to the hurting, afflicted, and uncomfortable. And so He does today. We must come to the end of ourselves. It is then that we shall behold Jesus Himself.

4. Ibid., p. 24.

2
THE NECESSITY FOR PRAYER AND AWAKENING

There scarcely was a single person in the town, old or young, left unconcerned about the great things of the eternal world . . . and the work of conversion was carried out in a most astonishing manner and increased more and more; souls did as it were come by flocks to Jesus Christ. . . . This work of God as it was carried on, and the number of saints multiplied, soon made a glorious alteration in the town, so that in 1735 the town seemed full of the presence of God: it never was so full of love, nor of joy, and yet so full of distress as it was then. There were remarkable tokens of God's presence in almost every house . . . God's day was a delight. The congregation was alive in God's service, in tears while the Word was preached; some weeping for sorrow and distress, others for joy and love, others with pity and concern for the souls of their neighbors.[1]

—Jonathan Edwards

"Return to Me," declares the Lord Almighty, "and I will return to you."

—Zechariah 1:3 (NIV*)

*New Internationl Version.

1. *Cited in David Bryant, With Concerts of Prayer* (Ventura, Calif.: Regal, 1985), p. 78.

This is what the Lord Almighty says: "Many peoples and the inhabitants of many cities will yet come, and the inhabitants of one city will go to another and say, 'Let us go at once to entreat the Lord and seek the Lord Almighty.' "
—Zechariah 8:20-21 (NIV)

When the bottom falls out there is only one way to look. That is exactly the moment God comes with power to His people. The inescapable fact is that we need God. Every great work that has been accomplished in and through my life has been preceded by prayer.

Little did I know that as Fred Bishop, Fred Starkweather and I were preparing to go to the Communist Youth World Festival, there were two men in East Germany praying. In the mountain village where they lived, they set aside a week to pray and fast.

The youth of East Germany had been turning en masse to atheistic teaching. The churches were left empty. The year prior to the Communist Youth World Festival, the elderly Pastor Bush had taken me one Sunday morning to a beautiful cathedral in East Berlin. But it was practically empty. Only a handful of people were there, and most of them were older than sixty. There were no young people.

The two laymen mentioned above saw the same thing happening all across their nation. After a week of intensive prayer, they began a youth meeting.

About sixty young people came to the meeting. The next meeting had 100 in attendance. It continued to grow until there were 1,000 in attendance. Young people came from throughout East Germany.

They decided to have meetings in five major cities. The meetings grew rapidly. After the Communist Youth World Festival, I attended the gatherings in three of the cities. In one location 1,500 young people filled a large cathedral. I had been told to be prepared to preach on the cross of Christ.

As I sat in this huge cathedral with hundreds of East German youth, my heart was thrilled. They began to sing with the joy of the Lord. The leader asked how many people were from that city. Almost all raised their hands. Then they asked how many people were from other cities in East Germany. A few raised their hands. The third question came, "Is there anyone here from outside the German Democratic Republic?"

Only two of us raised our hands. The other young man was from Hungary. Some people had met him on the street and witnessed to him. They invited him to come with them to the services, and I was serving as an interpreter for him because he spoke no German but only Hungarian and English.

The leaders had prepared me beforehand for the last question, "Is there anyone here from outside Europe?" My hand was the only hand raised.

The speaker at the pulpit asked, "And from where do you come?"

When I responded, "San Antonio, Texas," a roar of applause broke out.

When the applause calmed down, the speaker said, "You have come from such a long way. You must come and bring us greetings."

As I made my way to the platform, the crowd began to applaud. The greeting I brought them lasted close to an hour. After the service, young people swarmed about me. For well over an hour they asked questions about my relationship to Jesus. They hungered to learn more.

In another city the young people prayed for an hour before the services began. They then took their guitars and marched through the streets singing and inviting young people to worship with them. It was unbelievable.

I gave my testimony in yet another city where 5,000

young people meet regularly to worship Jesus. The cathedral holds only 2,500 people; therefore, they must have two worship services. I had never seen young people so spiritually hungry. Seeds of a great awakening are in East Germany. Those seeds were planted in the hearts of the youth of that nation solely through prayer.

The greatest ministry that any Christian can have is the ministry of intercession. It is this ministry that can turn the heart of a nation. The great soldiers of Christ throughout the ages have won great battles on their knees. It is on our knees that we see His hands stretched out for a lost and dying world. It is on our knees that we see the power available to us by a resurrected Christ.

Samuel Chadwick said, "There is no power like that of prevailing prayer. . . . It turns ordinary mortals into men of power. It brings power. It brings fire. It brings rain. It brings life. It brings God."[2]

Study the history of the church and you will discover that awakening comes when God's people pray. The Spirit of God is searching the entire earth to find the man or woman who will seek His face above all else. His nationality or race matters not. His abilities or social and economic standing are of no special importance. It matters only that he is seeking God's glory.

There was a man known for his ministry of prayer. John Hyde was even nicknamed Praying Hyde. After Wilbur Chapman had met Praying Hyde, he wrote a friend about his experience:

> I have learned some great lessons concerning prayer. At one of our missions in England the audience was exceedingly small; but I received a note saying that an American missionary was going to pray God's blessing down upon our

2. Lewis A. Drummond, *The Awaking That Must Come* (Nashville: Broadman, 1979), p. 121.

work. He was known as "Praying Hyde." Almost instantly the tide turned. The hall became packed and upon my first invitation, fifty men accepted Christ as Saviour.

As we were leaving, I said, "Mr. Hyde, I want you to pray for me." He came into my room, turned the key in the door and dropped on his knees and waited five minutes without a single syllable coming from his lips. I could hear my own heart thumping and his beating. I felt the hot tears running down my face. I knew I was with God.

Then, with upturned face, down which the tears were streaming, he said, "Oh, God!" Then for five minutes at least he was still again; and then when he knew that he was talking with God there came up from the depth of his heart such petitions for men as I had never heard before. I arose from my knee to know what real prayer was. We believe that prayer is mighty, and we believe it as we never did before.[3]

Praying Hyde was used of God in India. He became an example of God's using an intercessor to reach the multitudes with the gospel.

We need a host of men and women who will stand in the gap and pray in the harvest. This is not a glamorous ministry. The one who prays for the multitudes will never be known by men. He will be known well by the Father.

We hear of the D.L. Moodys and the Billy Grahams. But we seldom hear of common, ordinary people that have prayed for the great evangelists. In prayer those ordinary people have believed God to do extraordinary things.

In September 1985, Billy Graham visited Romania on an eleven-day preaching tour. The *Chicago Tribune* reported, "His crowds of more than thirty thousand were the largest for religious gatherings in that country since World War II."

The Crusade Information Service for the Billy Graham Team was even more descriptive:

3. James Stewart, *The Phenomenon of Pentecost* (Alexandria, La.: Lamp-lighter Pub., 1960), p. 40.

Well over 150,000 turned out to see and hear Evangelist Billy Graham on a whirlwind 11-day, seven-stop preaching mission in Romania, described by local officials and religious leaders alike as "extraordinary" and "unprecedented."

Huge throngs—applauding, singing, and chanting, "Billy Graham, Billy Graham"—greeted the American evangelist in the streets of almost every city where he preached. . . .

The crowds were the largest Mr. Graham has attracted in a special ministry that has taken him to six countries in Eastern Europe, including the Soviet Union.[4]

There was one aspect of Dr. Graham's crusade that will never be in the newspapers. God moved mightily through Dr. Graham in the large Second Baptist Church of Oradea, where Josif Ton formerly pastored.

Three months prior to Dr. Graham's visit to Oradea, I preached in that church on the principles of spiritual awakening. A layman asked in English if he could speak with me.

He said, "Friday, I was prompted by the Holy Spirit to cut my vacation short and return immediately to Oradea. I felt I needed to be in my own church on Sunday morning. And you were here preaching on the necessity and principles of spiritual awakening.

"I have been praying for revival in Romania for eleven years. I would like to travel with you throughout Romania and learn more of these principles of spiritual awakenings."

When he told me his name, I realized who he was. An evangelist friend had been to Romania a year earlier and said that he had never before met such a man of prayer.

We discussed with the pastors of the church the idea of his traveling with our team. They agreed. He could also serve as interpreter.

It didn't take long for me to realize that he would not

4. News release, Billy Graham Evangelistic Ass'n., 17 September 1985.

be learning from me; I would be learning from him. I asked him what he thought of the preaching of my evangelist friend.

"I have never heard him preach."

"I thought he preached a week of evangelistic meetings at your church."

He nodded. "When an evangelist comes to preach, I go to pray. When your friend came to our church, I gathered a group of men. We met prior to the worship service and prayed all through the service. As a result we saw your friend reap a great harvest each evening."

As we drove from city to city together, he often said, "Let's pray for this city and this country." Or, "Let's pray and fast today." He continually challenged me, "We must pray! We must pray!"

I never saw as many conversions to Christ in my ministry in Eastern Europe as I saw in those two weeks. The last four nights I spent in a major university city. Nearly 1,000 commitments to Christ were made in those four days.

The last night was one I will never forget. Every inch of the church was packed. Every available room was full, and people were gathered all the way out to the street. I preached, and my friend interpreted. We were both exhausted.

My message seemed to have no power. The people were there and hungry, but I seemed unable to feed them. Then something happened. My friend began to pray silently for me while I was preaching, and I prayed for him as he interpreted. After about ten minutes of ministering in this manner, I felt impressed of God to cease preaching and just quote Scripture. For about fifteen minutes I quoted Scripture while he interpreted. And the glory of God came down.

As we quoted Scripture people inside and outside the building began to weep. Hearts were broken by the Holy Spirit. More people were converted to Christ that one night than any other night of my ministry in Eastern Europe.

I didn't think we would ever be able to get back to the West. Hundreds of people gathered around our van weeping and praying and singing.

We left our new friend at a train station. He would return to Oradea. He said, "You have your ministry of preaching in the West. I must return to Oradea and pray. Billy Graham is coming, and I must organize the brothers to pray for the mightiest outpouring of God's Spirit that we have ever seen."

I drove all night through Hungary to Austria. I knew my life would never be the same. I had been with a man of prayer. Romania would never be the same again either; not just because Billy Graham was going there, but also because a man of prayer was already there. It was no surprise to hear of the wonderful results of Dr. Graham's ministry. He went to a country where the roots of evangelism were deep in the soil of prayer.

When the winds of revival begin to blow, there is always a wedding between the ministry of the evangelist and the ministry of the intercessor. They cannot operate without each other.

Jesus was both the Great Intercessor and the Great Evangelist. When He commissioned His disciples to preach, to win, and to disciple the nations, He told them, "But [stay] in the city of Jerusalem until [you] be endued with power from on high" (Luke 24:29).

In Acts 1, the church is praying. In Acts 2, she is preaching. In Acts 3, Peter and John are preaching. In Acts 4, the church is praying. We find this pattern throughout the book of Acts. The awakened church is continually blending the ministry of evangelism and intercession.

Charles Finney was perhaps the greatest revivalist in American history. He saw entire communities transformed by the power of Christ. Billy Graham has said of him, "Few men have had such a profound impact on their generation as Charles Grandison Finney. Through his Spirit-filled evangelistic ministry, uncounted thousands came to know Christ in the nineteenth century, resulting in one of the greatest revivals in the history of America."[5]

On October 5, 1824, Finney met Rev. Daniel Nash. Nash had experienced a deep work of God in his life, and he devoted himself to a ministry of prayer. Later, God blended the ministry of Reverend Nash and evangelist Finney in a marvelous manner in a western New York community, Evans Mills. The following describes the power of the evangelist and intercessor working together:

> There were a number of Deists in town who seemed determined to thwart the touch of God. The young evangelist met them forthrightly. He preached a direct and convincing sermon against their views. The result: practically every Deist in Evans Mills was converted.
> Not far from Evans Mills was a German community. . . . The Germans turned out to virtually the last person to hear the young evangelist.

Mr. Finney said, "The revival among the Germans resulted in the conversion of the whole church, I believe, and of nearly the whole community of Germans. It was one of the most interesting revivals that I have ever witnessed."[6]

Finney, throughout his ministry, relied heavily on intercessors. The ministry on the cutting edge of evangelism will always, always, be knit together with the intercessors.

It was intercessors who brought D.L. Moody to Europe. As a result, Mr. Moody would put one foot in America and one in Europe and shake both continents for God's glory. Mr. Moody went to England to hear the great preacher

5. Lewis A. Drummond, *The Life and Ministry of Charles G. Finney* (Minneapolis: Bethany House, 1985), foreword.
6. Ibid., pp. 72–73.

Charles Spurgeon and meet the man of extraordinary faith George Mueller. While in London he was asked to preach at the Congregational church in the north of London. He had come not to speak but to listen. Therefore, he reluctantly accepted the invitation. On Sunday morning he preached with little power and few visible results. He preached again Sunday evening and 500 responded to the invitation to receive Christ.

That evening resulted in the beginning of a great revival in that church. And D.L. Moody was thrust into a ministry that would stir the world.

When Mr. Moody told R.A. Torrey what happened, Torrey said, "Someone must have been praying."

"Oh," he said, "did I not tell you that? That is the point of the whole story. There were two sisters in that church, one of whom was bedridden. The other heard me that Sunday morning. She went home and said to her sister, 'Who do you suppose preached for us this morning? Mr. Moody of Chicago.' No sooner had she said it, than her sister turned pale as death and said, 'What! Mr. Moody of Chicago! I have read of him. I have been praying God to send him to London, and to send him to our church. If I had known he was to preach this morning I would have eaten no breakfast. I would have spent the whole morning in fasting and prayer. Now, sister, go out, lock the door, do not let anyone come to see me, do not let them send me any dinner; I am going to spend the whole afternoon and evening in fasting and prayer.' And pray she did, and God heard and answered."[7]

Many have heard of D.L. Moody, but few have heard of the lady in London who prayed. It is that type of person who can have a great impact on our world. Perhaps her peers would have thought that she had nothing to offer the church. Yet she had the most to offer.

7. R.A. Torrey, *The Power of Prayer* (reprint, Grand Rapids: Zondervan, 1971), pp. 36–37.

Many have thought that they can do little in reaching the world for Christ. Yet God is ready to do so much in and through the person willing to trust Him. There is a great harvest awaiting us. Jesus tells us that the first order of business for the church is prayer.

"But when He saw the multitudes, He was moved with compassion on them, because they fainted, and were scattered abroad, as sheep having no shepherd.

"Then saith he unto his disciples, The harvest truly is plenteous, but the labourers are few; *pray* ye therefore . . . (Matthew 9:36-38, emphasis added).

Prayer and reaping the harvest go hand in hand. Evangelism and personal witnessing are the vehicles through which the harvest is reaped. Prayer is the fuel that gives the vehicles power. When we fully understand this principle, we will be awakened to our responsibility of reaching the multitudes with the gospel. Some will go to the unreached millions. Many will give to reach them. But all believers must pray.

Andrew Murray, who wrote so splendidly concerning prayer, stated, "There is a Church, with its wondrous calling and its sure promises, waiting to be roused to a sense of its wondrous responsibility and power. There is a world with its perishing millions with intercession its only hope."[8]

Every believer must see the multitudes as Jesus saw them. Our hearts then will break. We will pray with the compassion of Christ. And God will raise up an army of laborers that will bring God's kingdom to the hearts of men.

It is to this end that we must pray. We must pray that His kingdom come and be established in the hearts of people throughout the earth.

Perhaps few have understood this principle as did

8. *Concerts of Prayer*, p. 39.

David Brainerd in the mid-1700s. Brainerd was used mightily to reach the Indians with the gospel. Many times he would be found in the snow praying for hours for them. He loved them with the love of Jesus.

In his diary he wrote, "I poured out my soul for all the world, friends, and enemies. My soul was concerned, not so much for souls as such, but rather for Christ's kingdom, that it might appear in the world, that God might be known to be God, in the whole earth."[9]

It is that kind of praying that will shake the nations. That kind of prayer will awaken the church. It will raise up a host of workers in God's kingdom and prepare hearts to receive His love.

9. Jonathan Edwards, *The Life and Diary of David Brainerd* (reprint, Newark, Del.: Cornerstone Pub., n.d.), p. 25.

3

THE SECRET OF PRAYER

A young man had been called to the foreign field. He had not been in the habit of preaching, but he knew one thing, how to prevail with God; and going one day to a friend he said: "I don't see how God can use me on the field. I have no special talent." His friend said: "My brother, God wants men on the field who can pray. There are too many preachers now and too few pray-ers." He went. In his own room in the early dawn a voice was heard weeping and pleading for souls. All through the day, the shut door and the hush that prevailed made you feel like walking softly, for a soul was wrestling with God. Yet to this home, hungry souls would flock, drawn by some irresistible power.

Ah, the mystery was unlocked. In the secret chamber lost souls were pleaded for and claimed. The Holy Ghost knew just where they were and sent them along.[1]

—J. Hudson Taylor

Call unto Me, and I will answer thee, and show thee great and mighty things, which thou knowest not.

—Jeremiah 33:3

1. E.M. Bounds, *The Possibilities of Prayer* (reprint, Grand Rapids: Baker, 1979), p. 101.

I had been in full-time evangelistic ministry for ten years when I began to realize some deep needs in my life. I had written four books and had been the subject of numerous magazine and newspaper articles by the time I was thirty.

It seemed I was at the beginning of a great future as an evangelist. I had seen many evangelists rise quickly as flaming stars. But just as quickly as they had risen, they were gone. I didn't want to be in that category. But something was bothering me. My ministry had grown larger than my character.

I realized that God loved me and wanted to conform me to the image of His Son. Though difficult for me to admit, somewhere in my ministry I had ceased to grow.

During the summer of 1977 I led a team of young people witnessing and preaching throughout Europe. Then my family and I spent a week camping on the Mosel River in Germany. It was great to relax with my wife, Tex, and our son and daughter, Dave and Renée. It gave Tex and me a lot of time to share our deep feelings with one another. God was speaking to me.

I had just read *The Life and Diary of David Brainerd*. I was so unlike that humble servant of God. I felt a tremendous tendency toward pride. And I knew nothing of the depth of prayer Brainerd had experienced.

I told Tex I wished I could pastor a little country church where no one had heard of me. Then perhaps I could have the time to develop a deeper walk with God. We prayed and placed our lives at God's disposal.

Within a year I was invited to become pastor of the Hahn Baptist Church near Hahn Air Base in West Germany. The church was made up primarily of American military personnel stationed in Germany. It was about as deep in the country as one can get. Hahn comes from the German word *Hahnchen,* which means "chicken." In essence, I became the pastor of the Chicken Baptist Church.

Within three years, I experienced a tremendous work of the Holy Spirit in my life. I developed some of the sweetest friendships I had ever known. But most important, I emerged from that pastorate with the touch of God on my inner being. I came to know a more intimate fellowship with God than ever.

Some could not understand my decision to leave my evangelistic endeavors to pastor this small congregation. But I wouldn't exchange the experience for anything. God had much to teach me. The first lesson was in the area of prayer. God had to teach me that *every* victory of eternal value has to be won in prayer.

One Sunday I announced that I would meet on Thursdays at 6 A.M. with any men eager to develop their walks with God. About twenty men began meeting with me, but the number eventually dwindled to about twelve.

I told the men that if we didn't learn anything else, I wanted us to learn how to pray effectively. As I reflect on those meetings, tears come to my eyes. The awesomeness and goodness of God was revealed to us.

Prayer partners were formed, and each of us began to develop a quality time alone with God. The more we learned to pray, the more we saw the provision and power of God.

We were beginning to learn how to communicate with the Father. I wanted us to learn how to communicate with men. I taught the men a simple four-step outline to share the testimony of what Christ had done in their lives. They were to practice by sharing it with their wives.

The next Thursday we prayed for opportunities to share with someone who didn't know Christ. Later during that morning I received a call from one of the men, Ken Leeburg, an attorney in a great position to witness of Jesus. Every person at the base who had a legal problem had to see Ken.

"Sam, can you be in my office at ten thirty? It's very important."

I arrived to find a man sitting across from Ken. He was an alcoholic, being discharged from the military because of alcohol-related problems. After Ken had advised him, he had asked, "Are you getting help for your alcohol problem?"

"I've tried all the programs, but nothing seems to help."

Ken took out his little four-point outline. "This is off the record, and you can tell me to stop any time. But, let me tell you what happened in my life."

To Ken's utter surprise the man said, "That's what I've been searching for. I want Christ in my life."

We prayed together, and the man gave his heart to Jesus. Later, Ken told me, "You didn't tell us what to do if someone wanted to invite Christ into his life. And I didn't think God would answer my prayer so soon." Later we would laugh about that.

The new convert's squadron commander was impressed. He asked if he could send more people to Ken. The following Sunday there were six new families in church, all a direct result of Ken's testimony.

Every man in our Thursday morning gathering had similar experiences. The church began to grow and eventually went to multiple services on Sunday mornings. The church won to Christ and baptized more people than ever in her history, and it was not because of some church growth formula. It was because men had learned to pray.

My wife mobilized the women in prayer and discipleship. Our goals were to establish small group prayer and discipleship meetings, to help every believer have a prayer partner, and to develop in each a private prayer life.

When the winds of revival blow across a church or community there is always a revival of the prayer meeting. People come together to seek God's glory. Wales experienced a remarkable outpouring of God's Spirit in 1904-1905. One of God's instruments was a young preacher, Evan

Roberts. Roberts was warned by a deacon at his church "not to miss the prayer meetings in case the Holy Spirit would come and you would be missing."[2] Roberts prayed for thirteen years for an awakening.

When the awakening did come, it was wrought and sustained by prayer.

One can sometimes discern the spiritual depth of a work by what it takes to get a large audience. In America we have bowed to the god of entertainment. If we want a crowd, we bring in a professional entertainer. We now even have musicians and comedians who see themselves as "Christian entertainers." They may bless some Christians, but this will not produce an awakening that will shake the nation. A politician fiddled while Rome burned, and he blamed the Christians. Today Christians entertain while the world burns, and we blame the politicians.

We must see that the battle is the Lord's. The enemy is not politicians, humanists, or liberals. The enemy is that "angel of light" who deceives the nations. He can be defeated only by the kneeling church. As the church bows to the lordship of Christ, "we are more than conquerors."

When I had traveled Eastern Europe, I met a praying people. I attributed their victorious living and spiritually awakened churches to their willingness to suffer for Christ. But there are also many places in Eastern Europe not experiencing revival. The difference is God. In the churches that are spiritually awakened, He is their life! He is their power! The God of Eastern Europe is the God of Western Europe and North America. He is no different. He is simply waiting for us to seek Him.

The victorious church around the world is on her knees in prayer meeting. In Korea thousands of Christians come together at 5 A.M. for prayer. When the church in the West

2. James Stewart, *Invasion of Wales by the Spirit* (Fort Washington, Pa.: Christian Literature Crusade, n.d.), p. 26.

begins to rise from her slumber early to seek His face, we, too, will experience revival.

We have developed a commitment rooted in comfort and convenience rather than in the cross. Churches are filled on Sunday mornings but Sunday evenings we normally find only a sparse crowd. And only a handful attend prayer meeting. Where are the men and women willing to wrestle in prayer for the souls of mankind?

Andrew Murray said, "God's child can conquer everything by prayer. Is it any wonder that Satan does his utmost to snatch that weapon from the Christian or hinder him from the use of it?"[3]

The church must be awakened to the power of this weapon. No dictator, government, or foe will be able to stand against it.

A friend who ministers in Eastern Europe visited a Romanian church. He and a team of preachers arrived unannounced for the worship services. The entire congregation was praying when the team walked in, and immediately the congregation began to weep and praise God. The pastor asked my friend to preach. He spoke with great power and saw much fruit.

At the close of the service the pastor shared with my friend what had happened. An American team of preachers had been conducting evangelistic meetings in the church that week. They had great success and saw the blessings of the Lord. However, the night before my friend's arrival, the secret police interrogated the Americans, sent them to Bucharest, and then deported them.

That left the church without an evangelist for the remainder of the week, so the congregation gathered to ask God to send one. Just as they were praying, my friend walked in.

3. R.A. Torrey, *The Power of Prayer* (reprint, Grand Rapids: Zondervan, 1971), p. 42.

There was great reason for weeping and rejoicing. This church had her eyes fixed on Jesus. She saw Him, a loving, wonderful, conquering Savior.

Rulers who try to destroy the church will be rendered helpless in the face of prayer. The praying church is the church that will invade Satan's territory and return with the spoils of victory. It is the praying church that will win the world to Jesus. We need congregations who make prayer a priority.

No one has written about prayer with the inspiration of E.M. Bounds. It has been said of him, "Edward McKendree Bounds did not merely pray well that he might write well about prayer. He prayed because the needs of the world were upon him."[4]

Jesus told his disciples, "The harvest is plenteous, but the labourers are few; pray ye therefore" (Matthew 9:38). Jesus knew that the secret to conquering the multitudes for His glory was in the prayer closets of His disciples.

I considered two men prayer partners at Hahn Baptist Church. They were Don Shelton, a deacon, and Ken Leeburg, the attorney.

Ken was a runner. He asked if we could get together a couple times a week to run. He wanted to be discipled and thought running might provide time for that kind of a relationship.

I agreed to run with Ken, even though I was just a jogger. He was much faster than I. I devised a plan to slow him down. We would memorize Scripture while we ran, choosing only verses that I already knew. While he was running he repeated the Scripture over and over. My strategy worked. It slowed Ken down.

The first verse he memorized was Jeremiah 33:3, "Call unto Me, and I will answer thee and show thee great and

---

4. E.M. Bounds, *The Necessity of Prayer* (reprint, Grand Rapids: Baker, 1976), foreword.

mighty things which thou knowest not." Many times we would pray together and claim that verse. We dreamed of how we could reach entire nations with the gospel of Jesus Christ. Then we dreamed of reaching entire continents and even the world.

When burdens became too great for us, we claimed Jeremiah 33:3. On occasion, the presence of God was so real that we would begin to shout praises to Him. The greatest and deepest friendships are born in prayer.

Ken had a hill that he loved to run, a steep quarter-mile that taught me a lot about prayer. It was so hard to climb that I called it "Difficulty."

When we would climb "Difficulty," Ken would shout in true military fashion, "Up the hill—over the hill—through the hill—conquer the hill—come on, Sam. You can do it!" Ken would be at the top when I was only halfway. "Remember the verse, Sam! You can conquer the hill!"

A prayer partner stands with us in the face of difficulty and encourages us to look up. He climbs the hill and tells us that God can give us strength to do the same.

When we come into spiritual agreement with our prayer partner, the power of all heaven is released. Jesus said, "Again, I say to you, that if two of you agree on earth about anything that they may ask, it shall be done for them by My Father who is in heaven. For where two or three have gathered together in My name there I am in their midst."

One of the most powerful preachers in the Western world in the last 150 years was Charles Haddon Spurgeon. In the mid-1800s, at the age of nineteen, Spurgeon shook London with his preaching. After D.L. Moody visited England, he was asked, "Did you hear Spurgeon preach?" He responded. "Yes, but better still, I heard him pray."[5]

---

5. Arnold Dallimore, *Spurgeon* (Chicago: Moody, 1984), p. 77.

The Western world today does not need better preachers. We need better *pray-ers*. Samuel Chadwick said, "The one concern of the devil is to keep the saints from praying. He fears nothing from prayerless studies, prayerless work, prayerless religion. He laughs at our toil, mocks at our wisdom, but trembles when we pray."[6]

It is interesting that the disciples never asked Jesus to teach them to preach. But they did ask Him to teach them to pray. Jesus taught that one secret of powerful praying is simply to pray in secret. "But you, when you pray, go into your inner room, and when you have shut your door, pray to your Father who is in secret, and your Father who sees in secret will repay you" (Matthew 6:6. NASB*).

It is in the secret chamber that we really get to *know* God. The greatest command in Scripture is to *love* God. When we love someone we want to spend time alone with that person to get to know him better and increase our capacity to love him.

Do you love God? If so, how much time do you spend with Him? Can we really love Him if we spend too little time with Him?

The King of kings and Lord of lords invites us to a private meeting with Himself every day. It is an intimate meeting of a good and wonderful Father with a needy child. In these secret meetings, we get to know the true character of the loving Father. And every day our love for Him grows.

But something else happens. We receive the touch of His character on our inner beings. We leave each meeting a little more like the Son. We are being conformed to His image. We seem to desire more what He desires and disdain what He disdains.

*New American Standard Bible.

6. Bounds, *Possibilities of Prayer*, p. 52.

This is true prayer. We enter the secret chamber not to get something from God. We enter to get to *know* the true and living God. And as we get to know Him we discover how *good* He is. The good Father blesses us with all the good things that we need. As a result, we have the joy and power needed to reach a lost and dying world.

Evangelist Charles Finney said, "Search the history of the world, and you will find that where there has been most true prayer, and the soul has been most deeply imbred with the divine presence, there God has most abundantly and richly blessed the soul. Who does not know that holy men of old were eminent for usefulness and power according as they were faithful and mighty in prayer."[7]

7. Charles G. Finney, *Prevailing Prayer* (reprint, Grand Rapids: Kregel, 1965), p. 46.

4
POWER FOR WITNESSING

And oh, how I loved my Saviour Christ then! I would have given all I had for Him! How I felt towards sinners that day! Lad that I was, I wanted to preach, and—

> *Tell to sinners round,*
> *What a dear Saviour I had found.*[1]
> —Charles Haddon Spurgeon

As we get to know Jesus Christ better we supernaturally-naturally tell others about Him. Our courage to witness comes from our knowledge of Him. Out of the overflow of the indwelling presence of Christ, we offer His love to others. It happens supernaturally, but it becomes the natural thing to do.

Following a border-crossing from Poland to East Germany, I well learned this principle of spiritual awakening. After the Communist Youth World Festival, I ministered in several East-bloc countries. Each has different laws and different degrees of freedom.

Although the Solidarity movement has been promi-

---

1. Cited in Arnold Dallimore, *Spurgeon* (Chicago: Moody, 1984), p. 22.

nent in Western news reports, evangelical Christians have more freedom in Poland than in other Eastern European countries. Crossing the border into Poland was no problem, even though one of our vans was loaded with musical equipment. In Poland we ministered unhindered.

I lectured our team early the morning of our departure from Poland. I explained the differences in the laws and border regulations in East Germany. We would have to be much more careful in our personal witnessing, if we even got in. The East Germans do not allow into their country anything that produces sound. At the border, they confiscate cassettes, video cassettes, speakers or anything else that produces sound. And they are thorough in their border searches.

Needless to say, everyone was solemn and prayed as we drove two hours to the border. When we arrived, there were two long lines of automobiles. The East German customs agents checked thoroughly every suitcase and every corner of every vehicle while we continued to pray silently and wait our turn. The guards searched everything in the car ahead of the van I was driving.

Finally it was our turn. The grim-looking soldier walked up to my window. "I have only one question for you." I prayed as I waited. To my amazement he asked, "How much does this van cost?"

I couldn't understand why he was asking, but I tried not to appear puzzled. "I don't know. We're renting it!"

"OK, you can go."

I couldn't believe it. He didn't look in one suitcase. He didn't even look inside the van! We drove through and stopped in a park a few blocks away, where we prayed for the second van that was right behind us at the border. Within two minutes it rolled up. The other part of the team had had the same experience.

We had a prayer and praise meeting. We had seen God's miraculous, loving protection.

We drove to the local train station for lunch. The place was full and there were no tables available for twelve. However, the East Germans have a custom that affords great opportunities for witnessing. A newly arrived person may sit in any free chair. So we split up and sat at about six different tables.

After we ordered, the team members were faced with a problem. Should they pray before their meals while seated with these East Germans after what I had told them that morning?

It didn't matter what I had told them. They had just seen the goodness of the loving Father. The supernaturally-natural thing to do was to thank Him for the food.

All of us did that separately, and it opened doors for each of us to witness. A lady at one table asked if I would pray for her. Her husband had been in an accident and was in critical condition. She was on her way to see him. I had a beautiful opportunity to share the love of Jesus with her. My wife, Tex, talked about Jesus to some young people at the table next to us. Other young people saw what was happening and wanted to hear and know about a personal faith in Jesus.

Someone was witnessing at almost every table. One of our musicians couldn't speak German, so he sang one of the songs that he had learned in German. As we left the restaurant, people continued to ask about Jesus. I prayed with and counseled several people.

When a person has been with the King, it takes more effort not to witness than it does *to witness.* The courage of the early church was a direct outgrowth of her prayer life. Acts 4:31 says, "And when they had prayed, the place where they had gathered together was shaken, and they were all filled with the Holy Spirit, and began to speak the word of God with boldness."

There are three ways in which we must get to know God, if we are to be effective witnesses of Christ. We must know Who it is that *sends us*. We must know Who it is that is *with us*. And, we must know Who is *in us* to give us strength, power, and courage for every situation.

Many people think I am courageous for going where I go. They think courage is part of my personality. Actually, the opposite is true.

Tex and I laugh when people talk about my courage. When we were first married, I was overwhelmed by my new responsibilities. I was now to be the provider and protector. I felt so inadequate.

One night we received obscene phone calls. I was so frightened that I put a dresser in front of the door of our apartment. Then Tex and I slept on the couch in the living room. Tex found out real quick how courageous her new husband was!

I am a chicken at heart, and yet, I have been to some of the most dangerous areas of the world. I have witnessed of Jesus in some of Chicago's most crime-ridden districts. I have been threatened by street gangs and arrested by the police. I have been chased out of one communist country and arrested in and deported from another. All of this happened while witnessing of Jesus.

It may seem contradictory to say that I am a man without courage, but in the natural, it is true. But when I know that the Father has sent me, I don't have to fear anything or anyone. The more I get to know Him, the more courageous I become for His Son.

Jesus said two things to His disciples about His sending them. First, He told them that He would send them the same way His Father had sent Him. Second, He said that He was sending them as sheep among wolves.

Neither sounded very encouraging to the disciples. Jesus kept telling them that the Father was sending Him to Jerusalem to die. Not only did He tell them about His cross, but He also told them that they too had a cross to bear. The cross was one of the most cruel forms of punishment ever devised by man. No wonder most of the disciples were fearful and not around when Jesus hung on the cross.

But, hallelujah! The Father didn't leave Jesus on the cross! He raised Him from the grave and gave Him victory over man's worst enemies: death, hell, and the devil. After the resurrection, the disciples no longer acted cowardly, but courageously. Peter the denier of Jesus became Peter the proclaimer of Jesus. The disciples beheld the power, provision, and protection of the loving Father. And that gave them courage to go anywhere He sent them. Almost all of those disciples died martyrs' deaths, proclaiming the wonderful grace of Jesus.

While I was at the Communist Youth World Festival, a young Catholic priest from Czechoslovakia heard me preaching and witnessing to the atheist young people in Alexanderplatz. He privately asked me to come to his country and tell the young people there about Jesus. He told me he had been praying in his home city and that the Lord had directed him to go to East Berlin to the Festival. He felt that he would meet some Christian who would help him witness of Jesus to the young people of his city.

This seemed a bit unusual. A Catholic priest from Czechoslovakia came to an atheist meeting in East Berlin. There he invited a Baptist preacher from America to preach the gospel to the young people of his city. However, after much prayer, Fred Bishop and I decided that the Father was sending us to Czechoslovakia to witness of Jesus.

We didn't know what to expect when we arrived a few months later. We rejoiced to see our new friend, who took us to his room and showed us a stack of papers. He had taken the little pamphlet "The Four Spiritual Laws" and translated it into the Slovakian language. He then personally typed numerous copies for us. "Please take these and tell the young people about Jesus."

The next day Fred and I went to the university to try

to meet students and discuss Christ with them. Fred spoke with two young ladies who seemed very interested. Both spoke English very well and said they wanted to know Jesus. After Fred prayed with them, they told him they had many friends who needed to hear about Jesus. They said they would arrange a secret meeting with many university students the next day.

We were so excited that we knelt in the middle of the large hall and thanked the Father. We began to sing the chorus "Allelujah." I heard people gathering all around us.

When I looked up, the hall was filled with university students staring at two Americans on their knees singing praises to Jesus.

Fred and I stood and began to preach. I preached in German and Fred in English. We continued for about thirty minutes until university officials questioned me in German before kicking us off the campus. Fortunately, my German was better than theirs, so I was able to avoid giving them information about who we were.

Later that night in our hotel room, Fred sensed that we were in danger. He didn't sleep all night and felt we needed to leave the country quickly.

I disagreed. "We can't leave now. We're supposed to meet those students."

Fred agreed to meet the two students, but only one of them showed up, and she was a nervous wreck. She said the meeting had to be canceled because the authorities had found out about it. She told us that we must leave the country quickly or we would be arrested. The authorities were going from hotel to hotel, searching for two Christian foreigners but did not know their nationality. She said it was just a matter of time.

We quickly checked out and caught the last train for Vienna. We arrived safely, only to find another surprise.

We had cashed all our American money into Czechoslovakian currency, because we had planned to be there for the rest of our stay in Europe. Eastern European currency is worth very little in the West, so when we changed our money back we were left with just a handful of dollars.

Also, we had special airline tickets from Frankfurt, West Germany, and we could not fly from Vienna.

We figured we had enough money to ride the train as far as Salzburg, Austria, and rent an inexpensive hotel room. Then we would be broke.

After a good night's rest in Salzburg, I didn't want to get out of bed. Fred had got up early and spent time outside walking and praying. When he came in he said, "Come on, Sam. Get up and praise the Lord!"

I looked at him as if he were half crazy. "Fred," I said, "we're out of money, food, lodging, and transportation. We're stuck in this city, and we don't know a soul. What are we going to do?"

"Praise the Lord!" Fred said. "The loving Father will take care of us, Sam."

A few minutes after I got dressed and we checked out, I spotted a wadded-up piece of paper on the ground. I picked it up and rejoiced. It was a West German 100-mark note! It was enough money to get us to Frankfurt so we could fly back to the United States.

God had taught me a valuable lesson. When the Father sends His child, He will care for that child.

"Lo, I am with you always, even to the end of the age" is one of the most comforting promises in all of Scripture. As a child I was frightened in the dark. However, if my father or older brother went with me, I knew everything would be all right.

Jesus sends us into a dark world, surrounded by evil and danger. We are the Father's sheep and there is a pack of wolves ready to devour us. The wolves are called Rejection, Persecution, Insecurity, and Fear. However, the Great

Shepherd, Jesus, promised to be with us. The wolves flee from the face of the Great Shepherd.

When Tex and I first began to minister in Romania, we met secretly with some university students every day in the mountains. We taught basic principles of discipleship and witnessing. One girl, Lydia, had a tremendous hunger for the Word of God.

One day Lydia had a fever. We told her she must not climb the mountain, but she said, "I must. I must learn how to tell my friends about Jesus."

A year and a half later I met with those same university students. They told me how brave and bold Lydia had been as a witness. I asked Lydia if she had a particular method. "Oh, no. I just try every day to yield myself to the Holy Spirit, and He gives me courage. One day I was witnessing to a girl in the university, and I thought that she was very interested in knowing about Jesus. However, I later learned that she was with the secret police. It frightened and discouraged me."

I asked Lydia how she overcame that fear.

With a smile she said, "The Holy Spirit who lives in me gives me the courage to continue."

5
MOTIVATION FOR WITNESSING

The wrath of God is like great waters that are dammed for the present. They increase more and more and rise higher till an outlet is given. The longer the stream is stopped, the more rapid and mighty is its course when once it is let loose.[1]

—Jonathan Edwards

But God demonstrated His own love toward us, in that while we were yet sinners Christ died for us. Much more then, having now been justified by His blood, we shall be saved from the wrath of God through Him.

—Romans 5:8-9 (NASB)

It's very easy to become so involved in the work of the Lord that we lose sight of the Lord of the work. Precisely at this point, we need an awakening in our hearts.

I had been a successful pastor when I began to realize that truth. God had blessed my ministry; however, there seemed to be a lack of the joy in my life that I had known in previous years. I struggled to understand this lack, but I

1. Cited in Peter F. Gunther, comp., *Sermon Classics by Great Preachers* (Chicago: Moody, 1982), p. 31.

could find no answers. I was serving the Lord faithfully and had no known sin in my life.

One evening I was in West Berlin with a group of friends, preparing to go the next day to the national travel agency in East Berlin to get a visa to travel in East Germany. My friends and I were praying when the Lord spoke one word to my heart: Availability. I knew that God wanted my availability more than He wanted my ability to preach and to serve.

I began to discover what God can do with us when we are simply making our lives available to the Holy Spirit to manifest the life of Jesus in and through us. Jesus is the joy giver. He is the greatest soul winner ever. We need simply to let Jesus be Jesus in us.

That night I asked God to teach me how to be available to His Son. The next day, after we made all the arrangements for travel into East Germany, we walked to a restaurant for lunch. As we passed a group of young people, the Holy Spirit quickened my heart. I remembered my prayer from the night before, and I said, "God, I'm available to You. If You want me to witness, I'm ready."

I began talking with the young people about their eternal destiny. At first they were shocked, but the more we talked, the more interested they became. After several minutes, I left them some literature and returned to my friends. Joy filled me because I knew that I had simply been available to the Father.

Because we were running late, there was a long line in the restaurant. A family in front of us kept staring at us and smiling and then whispering to each other.

I told my son, Dave, that I thought that they wanted one of our stickers that proclaimed, "I LOVE JESUS." He gave them a sticker, and they became very excited. They were Christians from a city in the southern part of East Germany who had decided to conclude their vacation by eating at this restaurant in East Berlin. It was an amazing meeting, and we became very close friends.

They asked me if I would come to their city and preach about Jesus. I have and many have come to Christ. It all began by simply becoming available to the Lord.

The Holy Spirit had me stop and witness to young people, which made us late to the restaurant, so that we could meet these beautiful Christians at the perfect moment. As a result an entire city was opened to the gospel.

When I returned to the United States I determined to place myself in a position of constant availability to the Lord.

It has been a most exciting experiment. On an airplane I witnessed to the wife of a medical doctor whose mother-in-law had unsuccessfully tried to witness of Jesus to her and her husband. She had told them, "I am going to ask God to send someone to explain to you what has happened to me."

And there I sat, an answer to the mother-in-law's prayer, telling this lady about Jesus. She wept as she received the gospel. Joy flooded my heart.

Many Christians are always asking God to use them in His service. If we will just make ourselves available to Him, our prayers will become, "Lord, give me some rest!" God is willing to use us more than we will ever know. As we understand this principle, we have a new motivation to witness.

Jesus becomes our motivation. The more clearly we are able to see Him, the more highly motivated we become.

William Nicholson's mother was converted during the Great Revival of 1859 in North Ireland. Nicholson himself experienced complete surrender after his conversion, which made him highly motivated to reach people for Jesus.

The turning point in his Christian life came at a Salvation Army evangelistic street meeting.

He described the experience: "As I walked down the

street that Saturday, it seemed as if every friend and relative I ever had were out and about. When I came to the open-air meeting and saw the two wee Salvation Army girls singing and rattling their tambourines, and poor Daft Jimmy holding the flag, I nearly turned back. Talk about dying. I was dying hard that night. I stepped off the footpath, and stood in the ring. The soldiers looked at me. Then to my horror one of them said, 'The people don't stop and listen: let us get down on our knees and pray.' What could I do? I couldn't run away. So down I got on my knees."

The crowd gathered. Nicholson could hear their laughter and jeers. The officers prayed. Then to his horror, she said, "Brother! Take this tambourine and lead the march down the street to the barracks."

"I couldn't let a girl beat me, so I took it. That did it. My shackles fell off, and I was free. My fears were all gone!

"That is, I lost my reputation and fear of the overflowing fulness of the Spirit. Hallelujah!"[2]

Nicholson was later used of God to bring people to Jesus in the British Isles, Australia, New Zealand, the United States, and South Africa. But he had first had to come to absolute surrender to Jesus before he could be His witness.

Absolute surrender of our lives does not mean that we are perfect Christians. It does mean that we are committed to being perfected by Him. The more we begin to think and feel as He thinks and feels, the more we begin to see through the eyes of Jesus.

The greatest need of this generation is to view life, the world, and a lost humanity with the eyes of God. The 1960s and early 1970s were years of radicalism and individualism. The late 1970s and early 1980s have been char-

2. V. Raymond Edman, *Crisis Experiences in the Lives of Noted Christians*, (Denville, N.J.: Dimensions, n.d.), pp. 93–95.

acterized by conservatism and apathy. The latter part of the 1980s until the end of the century must be a time of revival within the church. The population explosion demands that the church see the world through the eyes of Jesus. Militant, atheistic, communist movements and extremist Islamic groups have forced the church to her knees to cry out, "Have mercy on me for my apathy!"

We need a generation of youth and adults who will stand as a mighty army, saluting General Jesus. We must listen to Him and be motivated by Him. Then we must move out to win the world to Him.

There are three primary characteristics of the heart-beat of God that motivate us to witness of Jesus.

The lostness of man. The first is His awareness of the lostness of mankind. Jesus said, "The Son of man is come to seek and save that which is lost." In the Scriptures we continually see Him seeking out the hurting, afflicted, and tormented. Jesus had one goal for His life. He came to redeem lost humanity to Himself.

The revived church is always awakened to the lostness of man. That awareness always motivates the church with compassion to pray and witness as never before. During one of my most recent visits to Romania, the pastor of a large congregation exhorted me. "The doctrine of hell and man's eternal separation from God is very important to us in Romania. It is a motivating force in the revival movement."

One of my dearest friends in Romania challenged me even more. "Sammy, you preachers from the West very seldom preach on the subject of hell. As a result I sense a lack of urgency in your message."

I didn't want to admit it, but he was telling the truth. When I became a Christian in the mid-sixties, I was challenged by an ungodly hippie stoned on psychedelic drugs. I witnessed to him, and he said, "If I believed what you are telling me, I would crawl on my hands and knees and beg people to give their hearts to Jesus. I wouldn't be able to sleep until I had told somebody about Jesus."

The hippie's challenge struck deep in my heart, and God set me aflame for souls. My wife and I went to ghettos and drug hangouts to bring people to Jesus. Our hearts broke over the lostness of these young people. However, in the process of growing a family, building a home, and becoming a successful pastor, I lost sight of the lostness of man.

It took my Romanian friend to again challenge me with this truth. My friend encouraged me to re-read Jonathan Edwards's sermon "Sinners in the Hands of an Angry God."

He reminded me of my own heritage. "Sammy, your nation was born during a great awakening. And the preachers and lay people believed that man really is lost and that hell is the eternal destiny of lost man."

When I returned to the States, I read again Edwards's sermon. The Holy Spirit quickened my heart.

> If we knew that there was one person, but one of those that we know who was to be the subject of this misery, what an awful thing it would be to think of! If we knew who it was, what an awful sight would it be to see such a person! How might every Christian lift up a lamentable and bitter cry over him! But alas, instead of one, how many is it will remember these solemn reflections in hell! Some may be in hell in a very short time, before this year is out. And it would be no wonder if some who are now in health, quiet and secure, should be there before tomorrow morning.[3]

Perhaps we have not come to grips with this truth because we are a generation of positive thinkers. We have positively thought ourselves to sleep in a bed of apathy.

3. Gunther, pp. 39–40.

We must awaken! There are more people alive today than ever before, and most of them admittedly are without Jesus Christ. They are going to hell.

We cannot afford to sit in our comfortable pews, sing a few songs, and amen the preacher. The world is going to hell! We must break out of our comfort zones. We attend seminars and have fellowship and enjoy Bible study groups, but we forget that outside there is a lost humanity.

I think many Christians believe there are three categories of people: The saved, those who have believed in Jesus and received Him as Lord and Savior; the lost, those who have rejected Jesus; and the safe, good people who have not openly rejected Jesus Christ but have not accepted Him either. They are not saved, but they are not really lost.

This is error! *All* are lost without Jesus. If there were a "safe" category, then we should never tell anyone about Jesus. The moment they hear about Jesus and reject Him, they move into the "lost" category.

When we understand that all people are lost for eternity without Jesus, then our attitude about witnessing changes. The only hope for mankind lies in who Jesus is and what He has done for us. We must tell them that to escape the judgment to come, they must trust Jesus. The more we avail our lives to Jesus, the more we will set about "to seek and save that which is lost."

The love of God. The truth of the cross must become the most precious truth to us. On the cross we see that the wrath of God and the love of God come together. On the cross Jesus took the wrath of God on Himself because He loved a lost humanity. He took the punishment for our sin to satisfy God's justice. Oh, how He loves us!

It is that kind of love that makes us a unique breed of revolutionaries, revolutionaries of love. Divine love motivates us. It is the love that flows from the cross. It is the grace that pours out of the heart of God that enables us to love even our enemies.

When I attended the Communist Youth World Festival in the early seventies, I was often challenged by young atheists. They claimed they were committed to the masses of the world. I asked them, "Do you love Richard Nixon?"

Words of hate and anger came out as they screamed, "He's a filthy capitalist! He must be destroyed."

I would quickly respond, "That's the problem. The Communists love the Communists; the capitalists love the capitalists. The Jews love the Jews, and the Arabs love the Arabs. The blacks love the blacks, and the whites love the whites. The problem is that each hates his enemies. The Scripture says God demonstrates His own love toward us in that "while we were yet sinners, Christ died for us."

The Communists didn't know how to respond to that. They had come up against true revolutionary love, the love of the Father for a lost world. Even though the world hates us, we can love the world with the revolutionary love of the Father.

The awakened church will always have the world on her heart, because the world is on the heart of the Father. God didn't love just a particular generation, or a Western culture, but "He so loved the world that He gave His only begotten Son."

It is estimated that by 1990 there will be more than 5 billion people in the world. It is also estimated that by the middle of the next century there will be 9 billion inhabitants on planet earth.[4] Most of these will be born in Third World countries. Heaven and hell will be at stake with every one.

When the love of the Father breaks our hearts for such a massive humanity, then we will move into world evangelism. We will move with unprecedented power and force to win the 500 million Buddhists to Jesus. We will cry

4. David Bryant, *With Concerts of Prayer* (Ventura, Calif.: Regal, 1985), p. 108.

to God for the 800 million Muslims. We will find a way
through the Iron and Bamboo Curtains to win the more
than 1 billion people entrapped by atheism.

R.A. Torrey, speaking of John 3:16, expressed beauti-
fully the love of the Father for a lost world:

> Love is the consuming, absorbing desire for and delight in
> another's highest good. Real love is entirely unselfish. It
> loses utterly of self interest and sets itself to seeking the
> interest of the person loved. This was God's attitude toward
> the world. He loved the world, really loved it.
>
> He looked down upon this world, the whole mass of
> men living at any time upon it and that should live upon it
> in all times to come, and He loved them all. His whole being
> went out in infinite yearning to benefit and bless the world.
> And any cost to Himself would be disregarded if it would
> bless the world to pay the cost.[5]

When we are awakened by the love of the Father for
the world, entertainment, fellowship, and getting ahead in
life will no longer take priority. Our money, our time, and
our very lives will be spent to reach the lost. The love of
God is not passive; it is actively seeking to bless and
save mankind.

It is that kind of love that will cause the lost to respond in faith to wonderful Jesus. When the communist
leaders began to harass and threaten me at the Communist Youth World Festival, the Father spoke to my heart.
He said, "Love them with My love."

One man threatened to beat me. I told him, "I pray
that every drop of my blood will remind you of the blood
of Jesus that was shed for you. I love you." He became
angry and left. Immediately two university students told
me they wanted to know that kind of love. After I ex-

---

5. Gunther, p. 47.

plained the way of salvation, they gave their hearts to Jesus. The revolutionary love of God can change the world.

The glory of God. The one final motivation for witnessing of Jesus is the highest of all motivations. It is ultimately the purpose in spiritual awakening: the glory of God.

Revival is the manifest presence of the glory of God. Those who are to experience the glory of God are those who seek nothing but God's glory. When Jesus ministered, He had but one motivation: the glory of the Father.

One reason for the outpouring of God's Spirit in parts of Eastern Europe is the lack of superstars. It is unlikely that anyone will ever be known as an outstanding evangelist, Christian athlete, or leader of an evangelistic movement in a communist country. The Communists would never permit it. The target of persecution is always among the outstanding leaders. From one perspective this has caused tremendous problems within the church in Eastern Europe.

On the other hand it is a tremendous blessing because it forces the church to become a people movement rather than a personality movement. It is not the professional pastor who must be the soul winner and evangelist. Everyone must be a soul winner and evangelist.

Recently, I was in Romania. My friend from Oradea, the medical doctor who prayed for Billy Graham's crusade in Romania, served as my interpreter. The pastor of the church where I was preaching wanted to introduce me to his youth choir. After the introduction, he asked the youth, "How many of you became Christians three weeks ago?"

All but two of the forty youth raised their hands. My doctor friend had led them to Jesus three weeks prior to my arrival. My friend is a soul winner and witness of Jesus. He is quite often bewildered by Western lay people who don't preach or win souls. The great revivals of the past have always been movements of the Spirit of God touching not only the professional clergy but also the lay people. Every man, woman, boy, and girl realizes his responsibility to glorify the Father by bearing much fruit.

6

HOLINESS—THE ROOT OF GRACE

Every man by his own natural will hates God. But when he is turned to the Lord by evangelical repentance, then his will is changed; then his conscience, now hardened and benumbed, shall be quickened and weakened; then his hard heart shall be melted, and his unruly affections shall be crucified. Thus, by that repentance, the whole soul will be changed, he will have new inclinations, new desires, and new habits.[1]

—George Whitefield

There is a vital connection between soul-distress and sound doctrine. Sovereign grace is dear to those who have groaned deeply because they see what grievous sinners they are.[2]

—Charles Haddon Spurgeon

In many parts of Europe, wine drinking is acceptable for evangelical Christians. But the Romanian revival among Baptists began with this very issue. Romania's largest Bap-

1. Cited in Peter F. Gunther, comp., *Sermon Classics by Great Preachers* (Chicago: Moody, 1982), p. 82.
2. C.H. Spurgeon, *The Early Years*, ed. Iain Murray (London: Banner of Truth, 1973), p. 52.

tist church had its phenomenal growth only after the church body entered into a covenant not to drink alcohol in any form.

Josif Ton told me more about this covenant, and as he related the humble beginnings of the revival among Baptists, my heart burned with a desire to know more of the holiness of God.

Evangelical Christian groups in Romania—such as the Baptists, Pentecostals, and Brethren—are known as "the Repenters" by the secular world because of their emphasis on repentance at the time of conversion.

The center of the Romanian revival movement among Baptists today is in Oradea, a town in an agricultural region where there are many wine vineyards. The Second Baptist Church of Oradea was a sleeping giant. It had great potential but was spiritually stagnant. It's hard to believe the difference now.

The last time I preached there, more than 3,000 jammed every available seat on a Sunday evening. People stood in the aisles three and four abreast all the way to the pulpit and around the walls. The overflow rooms were crammed. Doors were open, and people stood outside in sub-zero temperatures. In another room away from the sanctuary, 100 people prayed for me while I preached.

However, prior to the awakening, the church did not even have Sunday evening services. The pastor at that time had a vineyard, and he and several church leaders sipped wine on Sunday evenings.

When that pastor resigned, the church called a man who was committed to prayer. At one point in his ministry this pastor was not allowed by the government to preach. During that time he gave himself to the ministry of intercession. After his arrival he immediately began to teach the church how to pray. He had everyone write a list of non-Christians, and the church began to pray specifically for these people.

This godly man also began to preach on the theme "The Repenters Must Repent." He preached repentance and taught prayer from December to the following June. Then the church entered into a covenant of repentance.

Every member covenanted to no longer partake of any alcohol. Also, they covenanted not to lie on their jobs, a characteristic of the people of that area. The believers committed themselves not to be conformed to the world. The Repenters repented.

The Holy Spirit was released with mighty power. Fewer than fifty had come to Jesus and were baptized in that church during the year prior to this godly pastor's arrival. The church baptized more than 200 people in the six months after entering into the covenant. The church continues to grow and has become one of the greatest churches in all of Europe.

We must learn that God is holy. If we are to experience the manifest presence of God's glory, we must repent. When Isaiah saw the glory of God in the Temple, he was driven to brokenness, confession, and repentance. Too many in the West desire to know the manifest *love* of God without the manifest *holiness* of God. We have lost the message of repentance. Now the church in the West is the sleeping giant. The church in the East sends a strong message: The Repenters must repent!

Many have attached themselves to the church without becoming "repenters." We have preached a gospel without a distinct call for repentance. But throughout the Scriptures we are admonished to repent and believe. John the Baptist preached and baptized with a "baptism of repentance" prior to the ministry of reconciliation of Jesus.

In the United States several years ago I was witnessing to a group of homosexuals. The leader claimed to be the pastor of a homosexual church and said that he had "accepted Jesus as my Savior" and yet continued in his homosexual life-style. He believed there was no need for repentance.

This lack of repentance is typical. Recent Gallup polls show millions of people in America having had "born again" experiences. Yet there has been very little impact on the moral fiber of the country. The great awakenings of the past have always affected the morality of the people awakened and the communities in which they lived.

The disciples of Jesus were first called "followers of the Way." Jesus was the way. When they decided to follow Jesus, they decided to follow an entirely new way of life. That is simple repentance, a willingness to leave the old way of life in order to follow "the way, the truth, and the life." Jesus says, "No man can serve two masters. He will love the one and hate the other."

Repentance is the liberation of the will by Jesus Christ to serve God. The will is in bondage to sin prior to conversion. Salvation takes place when a person realizes his hopelessness and absolute need of Jesus Christ as Lord and Savior. When by faith he receives Jesus, he is made a new person. He now has a desire not to follow his old ways but to follow Jesus. He is placed on a highway called holiness. It is a highway upon which he will travel for the remainder of his life by the power of God.

There are many reasons people come into the church today without entering by the highway of holiness. Many seek a feeling rather than the Lord God Himself. Charles Finney, the great American revivalist, said:

> Many excitements which are taken for revivals of religion, after all result in very little substantial piety, simply because excitement is too great. Appeals are made too much on feelings. . . . A tornado of excitement results, but not intelligent action of the heart. The will is swept along by a tempest of feeling. The intelligence is rather, for the time, being

stultified and confounded than possessed with clear views of truth. Now this certainly can never result in good.[3]

Two young people at the Communist Youth World Festival were converted instantly when they made this statement: *"Ich glaube an Jesus"* (I believe in Jesus). These two young lives were completely transformed when they made that statement. However, many people in Western Europe and the United States will say, "I believe in Jesus," but very little change, if any, is seen in their lives. What is the difference?

When those two East German youth said, "I believe in Jesus," they knew that they could lose their educational and economic opportunities in life. But they *really* believed in Jesus. They believed in His life, death, burial, and resurrection so much that they were willing to forsake all opportunities in this life in order to know Him and follow Him.

When someone in the West says, "I believe in Jesus," it can mean very little. It is usually socially and culturally acceptable to make that statement. But too often there is no repentance, no forsaking of the old life to follow the New-Life Giver, Jesus Christ.

The need in Western civilization is for holy men to proclaim Jesus Christ as both Lord and Savior. We need men who will not compromise but will call the nations to repentance. George Whitefield in 1739 said, "I love those that thunder out the Word! The Christian world is in a deep sleep. Nothing but a loud voice can waken them out of it!"[4] We need the courage, the commitment, and the message of the eighteenth century to again permeate the twentieth-century church.

3. Charles G. Finney, *Revival Fire* (reprint; Denville, N.J.: Dimension, n.d.), p. 17.
4. Arnold Dallimore, *George Whitefield* (Westchester, Ill.: Cornerstone, 1970), 1:18.

Historian J.C. Ryle listed seven characteristics of the messengers during the Great Awakening of the eighteenth century:

1. They taught the supremacy of Holy Scripture.
2. They preached the total corruption of human nature.
3. They taught that Christ's death upon the cross was the only satisfaction for man's sin.
4. They preached the doctrine of justification by faith.
5. They taught the universal necessity of heart conversion and new creation by the Holy Spirit.
6. They spoke of God's eternal hatred against sin and of God's love for sinners.
7. They preached that there was an inseparable connection between true faith and personal holiness. THEY NEVER ALLOWED FOR A MOMENT THAT ANY CHURCH MEMBERSHIP OR RELIGIOUS PROFESSION WAS THE LEAST PROOF OF A MAN BEING A CHRISTIAN IF HE LIVED AN UNGODLY LIFE.[5]

These awakeners continually cried, "No fruit, no grace." Jonathan Edwards believed that "every experience of God could be counterfeited except those with an insight into His holiness."[6]

An insight into the holiness of God will always produce a life-style of repentance. When one enters upon this highway called holiness, it does not mean that he is perfect. It does mean that he is walking down a road of change. Repentance means a change of heart or a change of mind. Throughout the Christian life we should be continually changed, or conformed, into the image of Jesus Christ.

The revival in parts of Eastern Europe is not a para-

5. J. C. Ryle, *Christian Leaders of the Century* (1885; reprint, London: Banner of Truth, 1978), pp. 26–28.
6. Richard Lovelace, *Dynamics of Spiritual Life* (Downers Grove, Ill.: InterVarsity, 1979), p. 85.

dise where Christians have no struggle with sin. Revival makes the child of God more aware of the holiness of God, but it does not eliminate the sin problem.

Early in my Christian life a godly minister reached toward me and asked, "Do you see the blemishes on my hand?"

I told him that I could not.

He placed his hand under a light and repeated the question. This time I could see them. Then as he began to move closer to the light, the blemishes became even more evident.

What a perfect example of the true nature of revival! As the light of the manifest glory of God shines in our hearts, we can see more clearly our blemishes. There is only one thing that we can do. Repent.

In 1980 my wife was planning to make her first trip to Romania with me. She was aware of the revival taking place there, so she studied God's holiness during her quiet time. One evening she confided that God was dealing with her life in a deep way. As we talked about the holiness of God for the next three or four days, the Holy Spirit performed a work of deep repentance in our hearts. As we saw the holiness of God, we saw also our failures of the past, of which we had not confessed and repented.

Although our marriage had never been in serious trouble, there were many areas that needed healing. We became more open and honest with each other than ever, and we asked each other's forgiveness for our many failures.

We repented, and God revived our marriage in a beautiful way. Many hurts were healed, and we experienced a freshness in our love. We committed ourselves to grow in the knowledge of God's holiness. As we have done that, God has kept us honest with each other. We have journeyed down the highway of holiness, and God has continually purified us. That journey will not be complete until we behold Jesus face to face. Then we shall be perfected. We shall be as He is.

One of the purposes of revival is to keep our feet on the highway of holiness until we reach our destination. Holiness is the process of being conformed unto the image of Jesus. Revival hastens and provides the power for that process to continue.

That process not only affects the individual Christian, but also affects our relationships with other believers. It is startling to recognize that all true believers are on the same journey. None of us has arrived or will arrive until that glorious day when we see Jesus. This realization should cause us to love the brothers and sisters in Christ in a new way.

This truth was made real to me on one of my trips into Romania, where communications pose a great problem. Messages must be smuggled in and out, and when a person is in the country, he must be careful when, what, where, and with whom he speaks. Many informers cooperate with the secret police. There is a great deal of room for miscommunication.

One of the leading pastors in Romania had been offended because of incorrect information that he had received about me. The information was not intentionally given incorrectly, but after passing through several ears, it reached him quite twisted. He responded by saying some things that offended me.

I was scheduled to preach an evangelistic campaign in his church, and I was very apprehensive. I arrived just a few minutes before the services were to begin, so we did not have time to correct our problem. When I preached, he served as my interpreter, but there was very little of the convicting power of the Holy Spirit.

After the services, we decided we *must* reconcile our relationship. We stayed late into the evening talking and praying about our differences. We met again early the next morning. Again we prayed and talked until everything was clarified and reconciled.

That evening, with the same preacher and interpreter, the Holy Spirit moved mightily. By the end of the week more than 200 were converted to Christ. The Holy Spirit could be released only when our relationship was made right.

As God's people travel on the highway of holiness, we will ultimately change our society. We will stand for social justice and righteousness. The Welsh revival from 1902 to 1905 changed the moral climate of that nation. Charles Finney preached against slavery in America. The message of revival will always call for moral and social change.

This is one reason God has used Billy Graham in such a mighty way. When many white evangelical churches had their doors closed to black people, the Billy Graham crusades were open to all. He stood for truth and righteousness before it was popular to do so. Had he not taken this stand, other nations would never have opened to him; they would not have respected him.

It is at this point that the evangelical church must repent. We have been so afraid of the "social gospel" that we have not always stood for social justice and righteousness. On the highway of holiness, we get to know more of the character of the Creator. As we grow in our love for Him, we learn to appreciate the beauty and dignity of all of His creation. That's why the Christian church must lift a loud voice against abortion and racism. And we must stand with our brothers and sisters in Christ in Eastern Europe in their struggle to worship freely.

However, as we stand for social righteousness, we must never allow ourselves to be manipulated by political groups. Political parties are not traveling the highway of holiness. It doesn't matter whether they are Communist or capitalist, liberal or conservative.

The basic reason the revived church must be careful at

this point is that change must be wrought through spiritual means rather than force. For instance, the whole character of the television and movie industry would change if the Western church experienced revival. This would happen not by the electoral process, but because millions of hearts would be changed. Our appetites would be for the good and holy rather than the violent and sensuous.

Many of us would like to force repentance on society, but repentance is a change of heart. Therefore, we must preach, pray, and live out our repentance first. As we change, there is hope for society. And if society never changes, we will continue to stand for truth and righteousness. Force was not the way of Christ. The highway of holiness can be traveled only by those who choose to travel it.

7
HUMILITY—THE SOIL OF GRACE

Paul was also branded by humility. Moths could not corrupt this God-given robe. He never fished for praise with humility's bait, but in the long line of sinners put himself first (where we would have put him last).

What a heart's ease is the virtue of humility—the great joy of having nothing to lose! Having no opinion of himself, Paul feared no fall. He might have swaggered in the richly embroidered robes of the chancellor of a Hebrew school. But in the adornment of a meek and quiet spirit he shines with more luster.[1]

—Leonard Ravenhill

Let every day be a day of humility; condescend to all the weaknesses and infirmities of your fellow creatures, cover their frailties, love their excellencies, encourage their virtues, relieve their wants, rejoice in their prosperities, compassionate their distress, receive their friendship, overlook their unkindness, forgive their malice, be a servant of servants, and condescend to do the lowliest offices of the lowliest of mankind.[2]

—William Law

1. Leonard Ravenhill, *Why Revival Tarries* (Minneapolis: Bethany House, 1979), p. 125.
2. Cited in J. Oswald Sanders, *Spiritual Leadership* (Chicago: Moody, 1980), p. 57.

My life has been touched by a group of young people in East Germany. After the Communist Youth World Fest concluded, I followed up the young people who made commitments to Christ. It was exciting to find that more than 90 percent followed through with their commitment to Christ. They became involved in local churches and youth groups.

I was ministering to one of those youth groups in southern East Germany when God touched my life. Fred Bishop and I were teaching principles of discipleship to thirty or forty young people. It was against the law for the youth to meet with a foreigner, so we met in secret in an abandoned castle.

At the end of the meeting, one of the young people approached me. "I became a Christian some time ago, but I no longer have joy. There are things in my life I know are wrong, but I don't know what to do about them."

I told her 1 John 1:9, "But if we confess our sins, He is faithful and just to forgive us our sins and to cleanse us from all unrighteousness." I asked if she was willing to confess and forsake her sin.

She said she was. And we knelt and prayed together. At the end she said, "Lord, please take control of my life." Then she added, "*Egal was es Kostet,*" which means, "No matter what it costs."

We finished praying, and I looked up to see every young person in that room kneeling and praying. Fred and I prayed with each individually and every one used the same phrase at the end.

One prayed, "Lord Jesus, come into my heart and make me a Christian, *egal was es Kostet.*"

Another said, "Father, please set me free from this habit, *egal was es Kostet.*"

I had worked with youth throughout America and Western Europe, but I had never heard Western young people pray; "No matter what it costs."

There is a cost to revival. It costs everything! Too many cry for the power of Pentecost but neglect the cost. We want resurrection power, but we refuse the cross. The cross means death. It means death to our ambitions, dreams, and desires. It means losing our lives in order that we might gain His life. Jesus said, "And he who does not take his cross and follow after Me is not worthy of Me. He who has found his life shall lose it, and he who has lost his life for My sake shall find it" (Matthew 10:38-39, NASB).

After we finished that meeting with the youth, we went to Czechoslovakia. Some of the young people there had been members of the Communist party at their universities prior to their conversions. Afterwards, they stood in communist meetings and gave testimonies of their conversions to Christ. They were now in prison. They had evidently prayed, "No matter what it costs."

Back in East Germany, I asked one of the girls, "How are you doing now that Christ lives in your heart?"

Tears rolled down her face. "I was the top student in my school. I cannot continue my education because I became a Christian and identified with our church."

I wanted to cry. I didn't know what to say to her.

Then a big smile came over her face as she said, "But it's worth it! It's worth it!" She understood what it meant to lose her life in order to gain His life. The glory and grace of God grows well in the soil of such a heart.

The primary characteristic must be humility. James 4:6 says, "God is opposed to the proud, but gives grace to the humble." The young people in East Germany experienced revival and God's glory because of their humility. They had become nothing so that Jesus could become everything.

Many believers today are fearful to discuss humility. Yet we must discuss it if we are to be serious about God's sending spiritual awakening. Augustine encouraged the church to set about getting humility as her chief characteristic. There is no way for the wind of revival to blow across the nations without humility in the hearts of God's people.

Here are four major reasons humility is of such great importance:

First, humility is a natural response to a knowledge of the holiness of God. A young Christian leader in Romania said, "Humility becomes my natural state *only* as I recognize who God really is!"

Isaiah "saw the Lord" and humbled himself. Andrew Murray defined humility as "nothing but the disappearance of self in the vision that God is all. The holiest will be the humblest."[3] John the Baptist said, "He must increase, but I must decrease" (John 3:30). True humility comes only as we allow Jesus to be all and in all.

Second, humility is the most exemplary characteristic of the nature and essence of Jesus. He is the truest expression of humility. Jesus was, is, and always will be God. And yet at one point, He emptied Himself and became a man. He was called "Immanuel," God with us. The King of glory became the servant of men. He humbled Himself to the point of death, even death upon a cross. There is no greater illustration of humility in all of history. We must behold Jesus! As we see Him, we will hunger and thirst to become like Him. And to become like Him means to be humble, meek, and lowly in heart.

Third, humility has historical significance in the life of the church. When the church humbles herself under the mighty hand of God, it results in dynamic growth, both spiritually and numerically.

The watchword of the great Welsh revival from 1902 to 1905 was "Bend the church and save the people!" On Thursday morning, September 29, 1904, a young Welshman, Evan Roberts, and nineteen friends went to hear an evan-

3. Andrew Murray, *Humility, the Beauty of Holiness* (reprint, Fort Washington, Pa. Christian Literature Crusade, n.d.), p. 42.

gelist named Seth Joshua preach in a nearby town. Joshua prayed, "Bend us, O Lord, bend us."

The Holy Spirit did a deep work in young Roberts's heart. "I fell on my knees with my arms over the seat in front of me and tears flowed freely. I cried, 'Bend me! Bend me! Bend us!' "[4]

Evan Roberts was a broken man. He began to live and understand "Christ in you, the hope of glory." He understood what the apostle meant when he said, "I am crucified with Christ; nevertheless I live, yet not I, but Christ lives in me."

Evan Roberts soon brought a message that would ultimately be used to shake the nation. The message became known as "The Four Points":

1. Is there any sin in your past that you have not confessed to God? On your knees to God!
2. Is there anything in your life that is doubtful? Away with it!
3. Do what the Spirit prompts you to do.
4. Publically confess Christ as your Saviour.[5]

The results were amazing. Within a year there were more than 100,000 conversions to Christ. The Liverpool *Daily Post* reported in December 1904 that there had been no arrests for drunkenness in Rhos since the revival started. Outstanding debts were being paid by thousands of young converts. Restitution was the order of the day.

The gambling and alcohol businesses lost their trade and the theatres closed down for lack of patronage. Football during this time was forgotten by both players and fans,

---

4. James Stewart, *Invasion of Wales by the Spirit* (Fort Washington, Pa.: Christian Literature Crusade, n.d.), p. 28.
5. Ibid., p. 32.

though nothing was mentioned from the pulpits about the evils of football. In this country which had a reputation for being "football mad," the train for taking crowds to the international trial match was found to be almost empty! The people had new life and new interests.[6]

The Welsh revival had even greater dimensions than the small country of Wales. One young Latvian pastor from Spurgeon's college in London heard of the moving of God's Spirit and left his classes to experience it for himself. His heart was set aflame for Jesus. He later returned to Russia, led tens of thousands to Christ, and was instrumental in establishing some 200 churches in Eastern Europe.[7]

What would it take to have such a revival in Western civilization today? "Bend the church and save the people!" And our individual cries must be, "Bend me, O, Lord! Bend me! No matter what it costs!"

Such humility and brokenness is a fertile field for the seeds of a great awakening. The God of 1904 is the God of today and tomorrow. This generation could see the greatest revival in the history of the church.

Fourth, humility is the biblical condition laid down by God for revival. It is the first step toward revival, according to 2 Chronicles 7:14. It's interesting that the flames of revival today are burning primarily in Third World countries. They do not have the technology or the organizational expertise of the West, but they do have the biblical condition necessary for revival. They have a simple and humble life-style.

Jonathan Edwards recorded the evidences of spiritual awakening in his treatise, *Distinguishing Marks of a Work of the Spirit of God.* He said there were five marks of genuineness in true revival:

6. Ibid., p. 64.
7. Ibid., p. 66

1. It exalts Jesus Christ.
2. It attacks the kingdom of darkness.
3. It honors the Scriptures.
4. It promotes sound doctrine.
5. It produces an outpouring of love toward God and men.[8]

Humility dispels darkness because it is the opposite of pride. Pride is the banner of the world. It caused Lucifer to be cast out of heaven. He is the prince of the world, deceiving men and women and building a kingdom of darkness with pride as its foundation.

J.C. Ryle stated that the language of the heart will always be that of humility with those who are used to destroy the kingdom of darkness. "Language like this no doubt seems foolishness and affectation to the world; but the well-instructed Bible reader will see it in the heartfelt experience of all the brightest saints."[9]

To understand humility we must know that it is not an outer characteristic but rather an inner attitude. Religious leaders during the time of Jesus attempted to impress people with their public prayers, fasting, and dress. But Jesus recognized *only* humility of the heart.

The man or woman with the most humble heart will never know it. It is impossible to become proud of your humility. One of the young Romanian disciples told me, "Sammy, this thing of humility is paradoxical. The moment that I think that I have found it, it eludes me." True humility is derived from a knowledge of God. The more we get to know Him, the more we are broken of pride and self-centeredness.

Humility is the most precious commodity of the church. It is more valuable than our buildings, our talents, and our programs. The church must have humility if the church is to have awakening.

8. Cited in Richard Lovelace, *Dynamics of Spiritual Life* (Downer's Grove, Ill.: InterVarsity, 1979), p. 42.
9. J. C. Ryle, *Christian Leaders of the Eighteenth Century* (1855; reprint, London: Banner of Truth, 1978), p. 57.

8
OVERCOMING FEAR

Johann Oncken's success was such that soon the civil authorities attempted to stop him, but he always seemed to find a way around their restrictions. . . . The police chief told Oncken, "As long as I can lift this little finger, you will feel the force of it." To which Oncken is reported to have replied with characteristic courage: "I believe you do not see what I see. You see only your own arm, but I am not looking at that. I see a greater arm, and that is the arm of God. So long as that arm moves, you will never silence me." Eventually the police chief ceased his opposition.[1]

—William L. Wagner

After the Communist Youth World Festival, I became close friends with many of the young people who made commitments to Jesus Christ. Several months after the Fest I visited a group of these who were mountain climbers from East Germany. They took Fred and Nancy Starkweather and me to an area of East Germany known as "Little Switzerland," one of the most beautiful areas of that country.

1. William Wagner, *New Move Forward in Europe* (Pasadena, Calif.: William Carey Library, 1978), p. 8.

The young people said that a person could look from the top of one mountain and see all the way to Czechoslovakia one way and all the way to West Germany the other.

There was only one problem. I have always had a fear of heights. They assured me there was a trail that would not be dangerous. I decided to attempt it.

The trail was nice, and the view was tremendous. About two-thirds of the way up, however, the trail ended. Then we began to *really* climb. We had to pull ourselves over rocks and make our own paths. I did fine until about fifty feet from the top. I could see for miles. It was fantastic!

But something snapped within me. I grabbed a rock and held on as a child would cling to its father in terror. I was frozen. I couldn't move. I was at the rear of the group and no one noticed me. When they arrived at the top they realized I was not with them. They looked down and saw what must have been hilarious; a fully mature American preacher clinging to a rock like a baby.

Fred Starkweather came back down to me. "Sam, what in the world are you doing?"

"I c-ca-can't move, Fred!"

"Sam, come on up. The view is tremendous. And besides, the East Germans will think Americans are cowards."

My body was immobilized. "I can't move, Fred."

By this time the others came down to find out what was happening. They assured me that the remainder of the climb was not dangerous and that I had nothing to be worried about. All I could say was, "I can't move!"

They decided that if I couldn't go up, we would all have to go down the mountain. But they didn't understand. "I can't move!"

Fred couldn't believe it. "What do you mean, Sam? If we don't go up, we have to go down."

True to form, I responded, "I can't move."

It began to rain. "Sam, if you don't go down the mountain right now, you'll slide the whole way."

It didn't matter. "I can't move!"

Finally, Fred and one of the East Germans pried my fingers from the rock, put their shoulders under my arms, and carried me down like an injured soldier. At the bottom we laughed and laughed.

Every time I think about that, it brings tears of laughter to my eyes. But I also learned a valuable lesson. I came to understand the tremendous power of fear. Fear had paralyzed me.

Fear has also paralyzed the Body of Christ. One fear that knows no boundaries, has no time limitations, is found in Eastern and Western Europe as well as in the United States. It cripples the church and robs men of the blessing of the Lord.

It is the fear of rejection. All people have a deep fear of being rejected by their friends and family members. In the East that fear runs even deeper. Christians may be rejected for sharing the gospel, and then they lose educational and economic opportunities.

The need for acceptance stems back to the beginning of human history. When Adam was in the garden with Eve, his every need was met. There was no fear. God walked and fellowshiped with Adam. There was perfect harmony.

However, when Adam and Eve disobeyed God, fear filled their hearts. When God visited them, they hid. God is holy, and they had become unholy. Since that day there has been a deep sense of rejection in the heart of sinful man.

Every person desperately wants acceptance. We try to gain acceptance in three ways. One way is legitimate; the other two are not.

People try to find acceptance through other people. A teen might try drinking or drugs. He thinks that will get his friends to accept him. After he has compromised, the sinking feeling of rejection remains. A girl might compromise her moral principles to gain acceptance. But after her sexual encounters, she is still haunted by rejection.

I have met husbands and wives who loved each other when they married, yet several years later they almost hate each other. How can this be? The moment that one feels rejected by the other, there is a feeling of betrayal. They thought that they had conquered rejection through the relationship, but rejection follows them through their lives.

Young people feel rejected by their parents, yet some of their parents are the most loving, kind, and gracious people anyone would want to meet. Even wonderful parents cannot overcome that deep fear of rejection. No individual or group can give us enough acceptance to conquer it.

Fear of rejection is there because of a broken relationship with a holy God. Many attempt to please God and thus receive His acceptance. Many become more religious. But in the shadow of their religion stands a tall, ugly figure called "Rejection." Many churches are filled with people working hard to escape this figure, but the fear of rejection can never be escaped by religion.

Revival always awakens man to the true basis of acceptance. Acceptance can be found only through faith. Martin Luther understood that "the just shall live by faith," and he shook the world for God's glory. He did not experience some new faith. He came to know and experience the faith of the spiritual giants of centuries past. His faith was the same as Abraham's, Isaac's, and Jacob's. It was the faith of Paul, Peter, and John. True faith is simply *our acceptance of His acceptance of us based on what Jesus did on the cross.*

Old Testament believers found acceptance by looking forward to the Messiah. We find our acceptance by looking back to the cross. One word gushes forth from the cross: *grace.* Rejection has to flee when that word is spoken. Hallelujah! I have been accepted! By grace I have been accepted! Sin separated man from God. But God entered human history uniquely through Jesus. He was unique. He was so much God that it was as though He was not man. And yet, He was so much man that it was as though He was not God. He was Son of God and Son of Man. He was the God-man. He crashed through the wall of sin that separates man from God. He has become the door through that wall. He forever stands as the doorway to God's acceptance. And when we have been accepted by the Father, we have really been accepted! That causes us to bow before the Father to love and worship Him in simplicity and devotion. He has met the deepest need of our lives through His Son, Jesus.

Revival always gives us a fresh glimpse of Jesus. Therefore, revival will always produce a deep sense of security within God's people. Three principles operate within the church based on our awareness of Christ's acceptance of us:

We have a new power to accept ourselves as we are. That enables us to accept others in a revolutionary way.

We can witness for Christ powerfully and boldly without fear of rejection.

But most important, we have peace and contentment. That security gives us the ability to stand alone. If the whole world rejects us, we can stand alone for God. We have been accepted by Him, and that is all that matters.

One of the senseless games the church plays is the pursuit of being what we are not. When God awakens His church, we become transparent. We have an ability to accept ourselves because He accepts us.

When I became a Christian, a tremendous personality change took place. Prior to my conversion, I was Mr. Popularity. I always tried to impress people. I could never relax and be myself. When Christ came into my life, I quit playing the game. I could be myself in Christ. I accepted myself. I relaxed.

After several years in the ministry, I found myself

playing the game again. I wanted to impress others with my abilities. One day my soul was awakened to the sufficiency of what Jesus did on the cross. I knew I no longer needed to impress anyone. I could just be who God made me to be. That released tremendous spiritual power. The power of my ministry is in the sufficiency of Jesus.

It doesn't matter whether we change a diaper in the nursery or preach a great evangelistic campaign. The only matter of importance is that we have submitted to God's will.

G. Campbell Morgan is known as one of the great Bible preachers and teachers of the past 100 years. On May 2, 1898, Morgan preached a trial sermon in consideration for the Methodist ministry. He was accustomed to speaking to thousands, but on that Sunday he preached to only seventy-five people. They rejected him. Morgan wired his father, "Rejected!" His father wired back, "Rejected on earth—accepted in heaven!"[2] Morgan later became a prince among preachers. He could be so only because he knew the source of his acceptance.

The last night of the Communist Youth World Fest was truly a revolutionary night in my life. Fred Bishop, Fred Starkweather, and I had been ministering in the midst of 100,000 hardcore revolutionaries. Theirs was not a revolution of grace but of violence and hate. During that week we saw 200 young people come to know Jesus Christ as Lord and Savior.

I met with a number of these young people privately for discipleship training. An elderly lady sat and listened the entire time. When the meeting was over she gave me a plaque that read, *"Wir sind doch Brüder* (We are truly brothers)."* She also gave me a small note pad, in which she had written Matthew 5:10-12:

2. Warren Wiersbe, *Walking with the Giants* (Grand Rapids: Baker, 1976), p. 170.

Blessed are those who have been persecuted for the sake of righteousness, for theirs is the kingdom of heaven. Blessed are you when men cast insults at you, and persecute you, and say all kinds of evil against you falsely, on account of Me. Rejoice, and be glad, for your reward in heaven is great, for so they persecuted the prophets who were before you.

I did not fully comprehend those verses. But I would come to understand them in an entirely new way that last night of the Fest. A thousand young people boxed in all of the Christians. They yelled and screamed at us. I stood and lifted my arms and called for quiet. As soon as the throng quieted, I began giving my testimony of what Jesus had done in my life. The crowd immediately became angry and pressed in on us. They hit and beat us. I yelled to all of the Christians to form a human train. I knew we had to get out of there before someone was hurt.

We pushed through the crowd holding on to one another. When I got through the crowd, I looked back to see how the others were doing. Fred Bishop and Fred Starkweather were at the end of our human train. Someone was hitting them, but Fred and Fred were laughing. It was amazing! There was no spirit of anger among the new believers. To the contrary, the joy and glory of the Lord was among them. I then understood those verses from Matthew. When men persecute you, insult you, hit you, and try to destroy you, then you are totally rejected by man. There is only one place to find rest. Our total acceptance is in the cross! Glory to God! The supernatural joy of the Lord becomes our strength. We are able to love those who have hated us.

Not only are we able to love others with a revolutionary love, but we also have the ability to stand alone for God. Early in the Christian lives of many of the believers in Eastern Europe, they had to stand alone with God. The most awesome factor of the cross is the loneliness of Christ. He cried, "My God, My God, why hast thou forsaken Me?" (Matthew 27:46). The Father turned His back on the Son. His disciples forsook Him. And He who knew no sin became sin for us, in order that we might become the righteousness of God. Jesus stood alone. He could do that because He knew the Father had promised to raise Him from the dead.

In the cross we have the power to be mighty in spirit. Through the centuries, men and women have died for their faith. Persecution has never destroyed the church. It has only caused the church to glory in the cross. It has caused the church to become mighty, and flames of revival have been lit.

The history of the church is filled with those who have died for their faith, yet there are more martyrs in this century than in any other. Many are martyrs of Eastern Europe. They have a message for us. The power of the cross is sufficient to enable us to stand alone.

A young lady, Vibia Perpetua, gave her life for Jesus in the amphitheater of Carthage, North Africa, March 7, A.D. 203. When Perpetua was condemned to death for her faith she reported, "In hilarity we went back down to the dungeon." Later she was stripped, forced to put on a net, and sent to a maddened cow in the theater. The cow attacked and gored her. Then she was taken to a young, inexperienced gladiator who finished the job and killed her. Before being brought to the gladiator, she told her brother, "Give out the word to the brothers and sisters: stand fast in the faith, love one another, and don't let our suffering become a stumbling block to you."[3]

The faith of Perpetua and those like her shook the Roman Empire. Where are the young men and women of

3. Sherwood Wirt, *Faith's Heroes* (Westchester, Ill.: Cornerstone, 1979), p. 25.

this generation who will stand mightily for God's glory? The need of the hour is a fresh glimpse of the cross. We need men and women who understand the words of G. Campbell Morgan's father: "Rejected on earth—accepted in heaven."

9
OVERCOMING APATHY

I cared not where or how I lived, or what hardships I went through, so that I could but gain souls to Christ. While I was asleep I dreamed of these things, and when I awoke the first thing I thought of was this great work. All my desire was for the conversion of the heathen, and all my hope was in God.[1]
—David Brainerd

I'm often asked about the difference between the underground and the official churches in communist countries. There are conflicting reports in the West as to the amount of freedom among Christians in Eastern Europe. Some say the churches are full and that there is freedom of worship. Other reports are of torture, imprisonment, and persecution of Christians.

The fact is that freedom of religion is restricted in every communist country, even though the constitutions of most of those countries guarantee such freedom. Communism is an ideology. Christianity is much more than that, but an ideology is contained within Christianity. The ideologies of Communism and Christianity will always conflict.

1. Cited in Lewis A. Drummond, *The Awaking That Must Come* (Nashville: Broadman, 1979), p. 92.

There will always be some form of persecution of Christians by communist states.

Poland, Yugoslavia, and Hungary have more freedom than the other Eastern European countries. East Germany does not have as much, but freedom there is not as restricted as in Bulgaria and Czechoslovakia. Romania is very repressive, whereas the Soviet Union is even worse. Most repressive in all of Eastern Europe is the tiny nation of Albania. The amount of freedom in any of these countries can change drastically at any moment with a change of direction of the political winds.

The greatest issue is not church attendance. Many churches are filled. Three major issues concern the persecution of the church: evangelism and church growth, literature distribution, and leadership training. All three enhance a powerful, growing church, and the Communists do not want that. They believe Christianity is a disease. They allow people to have the disease, but they forbid them to spread it.

Fred Starkweather and I once felt impressed of the Holy Spirit to test the waters of spiritual hunger within the Soviet Union. We planned to go to Leningrad and then on to Moscow to speak of our faith. We printed gospel tracts and learned our testimonies in Russian. Although we had no contacts, we were sure God would lead us to the right people.

In Leningrad, an official tour guide met us at the airport, brought us to our hotel, and told us he was available to show us the beautiful sights. Realizing he was secret police we said, "Thank you, but no, thank you."

The next afternoon we took a taxi to the Baptist Church, the only one in a city of 4 million people. It is an "official" church, and we were treated graciously. They fed us, and during the worship services we sat in a place designated for foreign guests. The church was packed, the singing was magnificent, and the preaching quite good. The message was biblical.

However, I would estimate that 70 percent of the people were more than sixty. Most of the others were quickly approaching that age. There was only a handful of young people. A frightening thought entered my mind as I looked over the congregation: *It would take only the loss of one generation of Christians to lose the entire Christian movement.*

Back in our hotel that evening, that thought kept haunting me. Fred and I walked down one of the main streets, and as I looked into the eyes of the Soviet people, my heart broke. They were no different from us. They were born with a capacity to know God. We must reach them.

Fred and I spent much time in prayer and decided to find the university campus the next day and witness of Jesus to students.

We didn't realize that the different departments of the university were located in different parts of Leningrad, so when we asked directions to the university, we were sent to the Linguistics Department. Praise the Lord! That meant that many of the students spoke English. But we had no idea where to go or how to begin witnessing.

We wandered through a large building until we found a student sitting alone in a large hall. We were excited to find that he spoke English. We gave our testimonies, and he seemed very interested.

"All my life," he said, "I have been an atheist. My parents taught me there is no God. My school taught me there is no God. My government taught me there is no God. I assumed that to be the truth.

"However, a couple of weeks ago, I began to doubt. I wondered if there might be a God. The universe seemed so orderly, I thought it could not have come into existence by an accident. I said, 'God, if there be a God, would You reveal Yourself to me?' And now I am talking to you. I believe God has answered my prayers."

He asked us if we had any more pamphlets. We gave him a handful, and he told us that he would be right back. Not only did he come back, but many of his friends also came with him. Before long the entire hall was filled with young people wanting to know about Jesus.

It was fantastic! Fred told a group about Jesus, and I witnessed to another group. Soon six KGB agents came into the hall and arrested us.

For the next eight and a half hours we were interrogated. Even that was exciting, because approximately every thirty minutes the police sent in two different interrogators.

We knew that deep within the interrogators there had to be a cry for the truth. We felt we were on a divine mission to make Christ known to them.

They never left anyone alone with us, but in the middle of the interrogation an official from the university came in. When two interrogators left and before the next two came in, he picked up one of our Russian gospel tracts. He looked around, folded it, and put it into his pocket. "I will read it later."

During our interrogation, we were threatened with imprisonment and told to write out confessions of our crime. I said, "I thought freedom of religion was guaranteed by your constitution."

They refused to back down and told us to write in detail our crimes.

I began, "When I was eighteen years old, a man told me about Jesus. . . ."

I continued my testimony of how Christ had saved me and changed my life. I concluded, "And Jesus Christ has given me a commission to bring His love to every person on the face of the earth. And if the person reading this confession would like to know Jesus Christ, God's own Son, you can. Call upon Him now, and He will save you!" I wrote out a prayer that could be prayed if the reader was sincere.

It wasn't exactly what they were looking for. I pressed them again. "What is our crime? Do you have freedom of religion?"

They said, "We believe religion is the opiate of the people. You, therefore, have brought opium, a narcotic, into the Soviet Union, and you have spread it among the Soviet people. You have committed a crime against the state. A drug smuggler would be arrested in your country. You have done the same."

I responded quickly, "Then you don't have freedom of religion!"

"Oh, yes," they said, "we have freedom. People are free to go to church, but no one has the right to spread that sickness among the masses."

We were placed under house arrest, threatened again, and finally put on a train. We were not sure where we were going.

The Soviets had taken all of our money and our plane tickets. They had accused us of spying. We prayed and committed our future into the hands of God. The farther away from Leningrad we traveled that evening, the harder the snow fell. We seriously thought we might be headed for Siberia.

That night I thought more deeply than I ever had before. Life took a new dimension for me as I thought of my family and of prison in Siberia. My thoughts raced back 2,000 years to when Jesus said, "Go!"

I asked myself, *If you end up in Siberia, and perhaps never see your family again, was it worth it?*

Out the window of the train, I saw soldiers with machine guns, standing in the snow. At that moment I remembered the atheist who had been converted to Christ at the university, and I wept. *It's worth it! It's worth it! For one soul to come to Jesus, it's worth it!*

I did not have to go to prison. Instead, we were deported to Helsinki, Finland. It was a great joy to awaken the next morning in freedom.

The Communists do not fear what the church does inside four walls, but they do fear what the church does when she leaves that building. But Satan doesn't need an atheistic government to hinder the church in the West from aggressive evangelism. He has rocked the church to sleep in the cradle of apathy.

The interrogators told us there would be no Christians in the Eastern bloc by the year 2000. But in the face of persecution and difficulty, the church in the East is growing.

My heart breaks for the church in the West. We could lose this generation if we continue to sleep. We must awaken. Our hearts must be set aflame!

Perhaps one of the worst errors in the Western church is the misuse of time.

I have been continually amazed that the church in the East has the ability to mobilize a large number of people on short notice. The first time I traveled to Romania, I preached in a major city on Sunday, but had no place to preach Monday evening. On Monday morning the pastor of the church where I had preached phoned a pastor in a nearby town and arranged for me to preach that evening. I thought no one would come on such short notice. The church was packed. People stood outside and around the windows, listening to God's Word.

In America it takes months of preparation and thousands of dollars to get that kind of a crowd. We have a different concept of time in the Western church.

Affluence and materialism have stolen from us that most precious commodity. Much of our lives are wasted before the television set.

Television in communist countries is controlled by the government. In Eastern Europe it speaks much of the time from a completely false view and therefore the church has not been captivated by it.

Many believers in the West are too busy either climbing the ladder of material success or reclining in the easy chair of home entertainment. We must be disturbed enough by the Holy Spirit to move out of our comfort zones. We must awaken if we are to reach this generation for Christ.

Two realities will arouse us: the threat of death and the imminent return of Christ. Most of us feel that we have plenty of time left. We have surrounded ourselves with a false sense of security.

None of us can presuppose that we have even one more day to live. And we will have to give an account of our lives when we die. Many of us will be embarrassed to say, "Well, I watched countless hours of TV." Others will say, "Lord, I made hundreds of thousands of dollars." God will say, "What did you do of eternal value?"

Ken Leeburg, the attorney in Germany I mentioned previously, was the best friend I ever had. He was not only my jogging partner, but he also dreamed with me of reaching the world for Christ. We spent hours praying and talking together.

Ken was a picture of health. He was 36 years old and had a beautiful family. I was shocked when he was killed in a freak automobile accident. Questions ran through my mind. Here was a man who loved God. He had a vision for the world. He was an outstanding Christian, a great husband and father. Why did he have to die?

It doesn't matter if we live to be 36 or 100, life is short. We will all die and give an account of our lives. After Ken's death, I determined that the sum total of my life would be given to things of eternal value.

The Scripture exhorts us to redeem "the time, because the days are evil" (Ephesians 5:16). There is an urgency about the gospel. The eternal destiny of mankind hangs in the balance.

Many Christian acts I do on earth I will also do in heaven. I pray. I will pray in heaven. I sing. I will sing in heaven. I serve God. I will serve God in heaven. There is one thing I will not be able to do in heaven: bring the lost to Jesus. It will be too late. My heart must be set aflame for the lost now. We must all be about our Father's business.

The other truth that should drive us out of our easy chairs is that Jesus is coming again. The last night of an evangelistic meeting in Romania, a young person gave a note to one of our team members. Hundreds were gathered around our van, and we wept as we pulled away from those precious people. A teenager reached in with the note. "Please, read it." It simply said, "Jesus is coming soon!"

Christians in the West spend a lot of time debating the theological ramifications of His coming. In the East they live in anticipation of it.

We need to learn to long for the coming of Jesus. Anticipate His coming, not by debate but by practice. We need to be on the streets, in the workplace, and throughout the neighborhoods calling people to Jesus. We need to live as though Jesus would come today.

Some may argue that Paul and the early Christians anticipated the coming of Christ, and He didn't come in their generation.

Yet Paul and other early Christians shook the Roman Empire for the glory of God. Perhaps if we anticipated the imminent return of Christ, we would shake Western civilization for His glory.

Awake, Christian! Life is short! Christ is coming! Redeem the time!

10
HINDRANCES TO AWAKENING

When . . . Rowland Taylor, Rector of Hadleigh, in Suffolk was stripped to his shirt and ready for the stake, he said with a loud voice, "Good people, I have taught you nothing but God's Holy Word, and those lessons that I have taken out of the Bible; and I am come hither to seal it with my blood."

He then knelt down and prayed, a poor woman of the parish insisting, in spite of every effort to prevent her, in kneeling down with him. After this, he was chained to the stake, and repeating the 51st Psalm, and crying to God, "Merciful Father, for Jesus Christ's sake, receive my soul into Thy hands," stood quietly amidst the flames without crying or moving, till one of the guards dashed out his brains with a halberd. And so then this good old Suffolk incumbent passed away.[1]

—J.C. Ryle

With all our technology and wealth, why don't we have awakening in the West? We have people concerned for revival. We have some of the finest Bible preachers and teachers the church has ever known. There is even a great prayer movement in the West.

1. J. C. Ryle, *Five English Reformers* (1890; reprint, London: Banner of Truth, 1981), p. 14.

We are in a battle for the souls of mankind. We war against Satan and all of the forces of evil in the universe. Satan has established his kingdom in the hearts of men and women. That kingdom must be destroyed and Christ's kingdom established, no small task for the church. But it can be accomplished.

One weapon God has placed within the church that can tear down the strongholds of Satan was used mightily in both the Old and New Testaments and throughout the history of the church. It is the life that is totally yielded to God. That person holds nothing dear to himself except Jesus and His glory. That life will contradict the culture of the day.

God is looking for men and women who will not be conformed to society but rather transformed by the Holy Spirit into the image of Jesus. This life will cry out, "I want Jesus more than I want anything!" Where are the men and women in the West willing to lose everything to gain God's glory on earth?

Too many of us think we can have God's glory at little or no cost. We live in a capitalistic society that guarantees our freedom. We equate our system with our Christianity. But the life yielded to God will cut across the grain of society. Capitalism and Christianity are not the same.

This truth infuriates many. But we must realize that an atheistic capitalist is no different than an atheistic Communist. Jesus did not come to establish a system. He came to estabish His rule in the hearts of mankind.

Many Latin American church leaders have been swept into "liberation theology." This theology offers political solutions to the problems of man. Revolution is equated with the second coming of Christ. The Spirit of God can never manifest His glory in such teaching. It is a theology rooted in human effort and struggle rather than God's grace. It is the result of a political-cultural dilemma rather than a biblical mandate. When the Holy Spirit comes, He always guides the church into biblical truth.

"Liberation theology" is a great hindrance to awakening in Third World countries, but the church in the West has its own form of capitalistic Christianity, and this also has become a hindrance to revival.

Western Europe and North America are the wealthiest societies known to man. We have been blessed by God. Much of our wealth and freedom are a result of our ancestors' following biblical principles. But we are in danger of worshiping the blessings of God rather than the God of the blessings.

It is difficult for Christians in the West to understand this. Most of us have never seen God's glory manifested among a poor group of people. Eastern European Christians have seen God's glory; however, they have little or no wealth or freedom. Yet they are free in Christ and rich in the grace of God.

Our tendency is to seek miracles rather than God. We seek to bask in the comfort of blessings rather than focus on "the old rugged cross, the emblem of suffering and shame."

We need to lay at the foot of the cross our most precious possessions. We cannot cling to family or friends or blessings.

When I became a pastor in Germany, I purposed in my heart to get to know God intimately no matter what the price. The first Sunday morning, I began preaching through Genesis. For close to three years I preached through that book. The Word of God came alive to me in a fresh way. After approximately one year in Germany, I came to a life-changing place in my preaching.

I was scheduled to preach on Abraham's offering Isaac as a sacrifice. It was a difficult passage. I lay awake Friday evening thinking about it as everyone else in the house slept. Suddenly I heard a noise in Dave's room.

I hurried and turned on the light. Dave's eyes had rolled back in his head and his body was in convulsions. I yelled for Tex and we held him, not knowing what to do. We prayed and wept as we rushed him to the hospital. The doctor on duty was a man I had been discipling. He found one side of Dave partially paralyzed.

He admitted him and stayed up with me most of the night. We prayed together. I told him what I was to preach Sunday and that I didn't think I could do it.

Abraham had waited so many years for a son and then God had provided one miraculously. Abraham must have been proud of that boy. When he introduced Isaac to his friends, he would have said, "This is my boy that I told you about, my miracle-child. God gave him to Sarah and me. He is the greatest blessing of our lives."

It is possible, however, that Abraham became attached to the blessing rather than the Blesser. And the Blesser said, "Give up the blessing." When Abraham became willing to do that, God sent revival to Abraham. Not only did God Himself provide a sacrifice, but He also fulfilled His promises through Isaac.

As a parent I know that Abraham went through tremendous agony. He had to be willing to give up that precious son. That was precisely where God was bringing me. Revival is often born from the seeds of suffering.

For the next year and a half, my wife and I walked through one of the most difficult periods of our lives. The doctors put Dave on medication, and he would do well for a brief period. Then he would react to the medication. The doctors would change the medication, and the same thing happened again and again. While we were struggling with the health of our son, God blessed our church. We experienced phenomenal growth. On the other hand, God seemed silent when we sought Him in prayer for our son.

We asked God to heal him; there was no healing. Eventually we had to return to the United States for medical treatment. After two years in the States, God had restored our son through medical doctors. I was left with a dilemma. My heart broke for Europe. I desired to reach its masses for Christ. But now there was a fear in my heart, the fear of losing one of the most precious blessings of my life, my only son.

I attended an evangelism conference in Texas and sat alone in the top row of the huge auditorium. I wanted God to speak to my heart. I needed to hear from Him. It was now three years since I had ministered in Europe. I wanted so badly to be there, but still I struggled with fear.

As I sat there, a long-time friend, Arthur Blessitt, walked in and sat in front of me. We talked a long time. Finally, he told me, "Sammy, you have a ministry to the masses. Jesus died for the masses. You must give your son back to God. You must give this fear to God."

I left knowing that God had spoken to me. The next day I ran into Leo Humphrey, the man who had taught me to win souls to Jesus many years earlier. I had not seen him in years, but I had heard that his son, Kelly, was dying of cancer.

I asked Leo how he was coping.

"Sammy, I have gone through the gamut of emotions. I felt guilt. I thought maybe there was some sin I had committed that had caused Kelly's sickness. I prayed for his healing. But he became worse.

"But, Sammy, I have seen the glory of God in all this. Several nurses have come to know Christ through Kelly's witness. Every time I'm with him, he says, 'Dad, let's pray.' He's so close to Jesus.

"One day I was pacing in front of his hospital room. Kelly called me and said, 'Dad, you are afraid to go to Central America to preach. You're afraid that if you go, I will die. Daddy, you must go.' Sammy, I had to give Kelly back to God that day."

Leo looked at me with an understanding smile. "Sammy,

I was with Arthur today. He told me about your son. You must place him in God's hand. Trust him to God."

I knew what I had to do. I prayed and gave the greatest blessing of my life back to God. I gave Him my family—my wife, my son, and my daughter. The moment I did that, I knew I had to return to Romania. I had promised that I would return. But fear of losing my son had captured me. Now I was free. I knew the Father loved my family more than I did. I had to trust Him, no matter what.

Later that day, I gathered the family and told them what had happened. We prayed, and each of us gave the other back to the Lord. We began to make preparations to return to Romania.

Within a year and a half I returned with my family to Romania. It was their first time to travel with me extensively in Eastern Europe. It made a tremendous difference in the ministry. I was no longer just a visiting preacher; I was a friend. Tex, Dave, and Renée made that difference.

We ministered in several churches. We then went to a remote area in the mountains and spent a week discipling university students. On Saturday we broke camp and headed toward a major university city where I was to preach Sunday morning on "The Joy of the Lord."

While traveling, Dave became ill with a high temperature. I knew I was about to enter a tremendous test of faith. Later in our hotel room, Tex woke me. Dave's fever was too high. He was dehydrating. In the middle of the night we took him to the hospital.

The hospital looked more like an old run-down hotel than a medical facility. Dave's room was even worse. Several beds were pushed close together. The doctors would not let me stay with Dave. Only Tex was allowed to stay.

I went back to the hotel at about 2:30 A.M. but I didn't sleep. I prayed through the night. I was away from friends, my church, any source of human help. I had to trust God.

It was even more difficult for Tex. Dave was rushed to another hospital, but she couldn't understand the language and had little idea what was going on.

At 9:00 A.M. I left for the church. I was drained. I prayed, "God, I gave You my family. I trust You now with them." When I arrived, the place was packed. Everyone was crying. One by one, they stood to pray and weep.

I asked the interpreter what was happening. "Sammy, God is doing something very special. There has not been a tear shed in this church in three years. But they have been told about your son. They are weeping for him. They cannot believe that you would come from the West where life is so comfortable. And now your son is suffering. They have identified with his suffering. God is touching their hearts."

God knit the hearts of my family with the hearts of that church that day. After church Dave was released from the hospital. The believers took care of him until he recovered. They asked me to come back the next year to preach an evangelistic campaign, something they had not had in many years. When we came back a year later, we saw one of the greatest movings of God's Spirit in our ministry. More than 1,000 made commitments to Christ.

The character of Christ is learned more in the school of suffering than in any university. God is more interested in building our characters than He is in building our ministries. A truly fruitful ministry grows only in the soil of a life like Jesus.

If we are to experience continuous revival, we must be willing to walk through the valley of the shadow of death. We will taste suffering, pain, and sorrow. God moved mightily in the early church. Thousands were converted to Christ. Jerusalem was ablaze with the Word of God. The fellowship of God's people with God and one another must have been sweet. But God never intended that the church should just have good fellowship. God intended that the church should win the world. They would have to break out of their comfortable, spiritual setting. God scattered the church by sending persecution.

Men and women who have been fruitful in the kingdom of God have always been willing to risk everything for the sake of the gospel. They risked health, wealth, comfort, and other earthly blessings to see souls saved. Charles Haddon Spurgeon was used of God mightily in his generation. He pastored the largest Baptist church in the world at the time.

Spurgeon shook London for the glory of God. When D.L. Moody was in Glasgow in 1873, Spurgeon invited him to come to London and preach in his tabernacle. But Moody responded in a letter: "I consider it a great honour to be invited; and, in fact, I should consider it an honour to black your boots; but to preach to your people would be out of the question. If they will not turn to God under your preaching, neither will they be persuaded, though one rose from the dead."[2]

Spurgeon was mighty with God and mighty with man. Where did he find his spiritual power? One biographer wrote, "Spurgeon was in no respect ordinary. He was great as a man; great as a theologian; great as a preacher; great in private with God; and great in public with his fellow men. He was well versed in three things which, according to Luther make a minister: temptation, meditation, and prayer. *The school of suffering was one in which he was deeply taught.*"[3]

This generation parades preachers and teachers promising health, wealth, and wisdom to all who follow Jesus. The only place in the world where that kind of teaching

2. Arnold Dallimore, *Spurgeon* (Chicago: Moody, 1984), p. 165.
3. Ibid., p. 176.

could gain a foothold is in a capitalistic society. One friend in the West told me that if Christians in communist countries trusted God, they would be wealthier and healthier. Third World Christians laugh at such teaching. When they choose Jesus, they choose poverty because of lost job opportunities.

However, they find themselves wealthy in things of eternal value and, in many cases, much more healthy spiritually.

I taught a group of university students in East Germany on the doctrine of godly suffering. One of them told me, "You are the first American to come here and teach that it will cost something to follow Jesus." I was embarrassed and ashamed to hear that my fellow countrymen went to such a place with a message of health and wealth.

Now, there is nothing intrinsically wrong with health and wealth. There are many godly people in Scripture and throughout history who were wealthy. But their wealth and health were not equated with their spirituality.

Also, they were not the owners of their wealth. If God blesses a person with millions worth of possessions, he is not then a millionaire. Rather he is steward of God's millions. That throws an entirely different light on our material blessings. Our joy is no longer in our abundance, but in Jesus.

If I manage much for the King, I am happy. If I manage little for the King, I am happy. If I die on the battlefield for the King, I am happy.

I am happy simply because I am a servant of the King.

11

TRUE WORSHIP—THE PRODUCT
OF AWAKENING

*Psalms are sweet for every age, and they create a bond of
unity when the whole people raise their voice in one choir.*[1]
—Ambrose, Bishop of Milan

*He who despises music, as do all the fanatics, does not
please me. Music is a gift of God, not a gift of men. . . . After
theology, I accord to music the highest place and greatest honour.*[2]
—Martin Luther

While preaching in Warsaw, I was invited to a small
village in eastern Poland, close to the Soviet border. It had
seen a spiritual awakening many years earlier, but the
church had never received foreign guests.

We arrived a couple of hours prior to the worship
services. The building was an old wooden structure with a
padlock on it. I peeked in the windows, and it appeared

---

1. Cited in Jane Smith and Betty Carlson, *A Gift of Music*, 2d ed.
   (Westchester, Ill.: Crossway, 1984), p. 15.
2. Cited in ibid., p. 18.

the room could hold 100-150 people. I walked around the village while we waited for someone to unlock the church. I was a little concerned about the attendance. There were only six houses in the entire village!

Everything seemed quiet (almost dead) in this little village. The only excitement was on the top of a telephone pole where a stork had built a huge nest and flew back and forth to it. I wandered down the highway to the edge of the village. I found a stream and spent some time in prayer there. Across the fields I could see the Soviet Union. My heart ached for that nation. I asked God to let me preach His salvation again one day to the Soviet people. I remembered the hunger for the gospel of the students at the university in Leningrad.

I stood staring into the Soviet Union when Tex came up behind me. "It's time for the worship service. Everyone is looking for you."

The church was full. I couldn't understand where they had all come from. Seventy-five percent were older than fifty. People stood at the doors and outside. Their faces glowed all during the service. It was easy to tell that these people had known the glory of God in their midst. We had a beautiful time of worship together.

No one wanted to leave, but we had a problem. We had only one interpreter, and he became involved with one of the members of the church. The people could not communicate with us. It was hilarious to see all our hand motions, like playing charades for real. Then one little old lady began to sing "How Great Thou Art" in Polish. They sang a verse, and we sang a verse. Then they began "The Old Rugged Cross." The communication barrier was broken. They communicated clearly with us. They loved Jesus more than anything in this world.

Later that week we traveled to the opposite side of the nation and ministered in a church in a major city near the East German border. Seventy-five percent of those people were under thirty, and although this church was metropolitan in nature, it had several of the same characteristics as the little country church. They, too, had experienced the touch of God.

The church was full. And they loved to sing. Someone had brought them many short praise and Scripture choruses. The joy and love of Jesus on their faces were the same as we had seen in the little country church.

The fruit of revival is the same all over the world. It doesn't matter whether the revival is among young or old, educated or illiterate; the fruit remains the same.

I have found six characteristics of worship among those experiencing revival. I confess I am not a musician, but as one who has worshiped with those who have a fresh touch of God upon their lives, I know that when God touches the heart, a new song flows from the lips.

So, first, revival is the result of a fresh knowledge of God, and the revived need an expression of worship for the true and living God.

George Frederic Handel wrote the *Messiah* in twenty-four days without leaving his house. His servant brought him food, but he would often find it untouched. Once the servant found Handel weeping as he wrote the "Hallelujah Chorus." Handel cried, "I did think I did see all Heaven before me, and the great God Himself!"[3] The dynamic of that masterpiece revealed the nature of God's character to the composer.

Second, the only motive of true worship is the glory of God. One of the great blessings of my life has been to sit in the worship service of an Eastern European church that has experienced revival. The congregation sings with magnificent power. I can see smiling, joyful faces, men and women weeping as they sing about the love of God. They are in no way passive. They desire only to glorify God as they praise Him.

A group of young people traveled with me in Roma-

3. Ibid., p. 59.

nia, translating Scripture choruses and singing them to congregations where I preached. They sang and then gave testimonies. God moved mightily in the services where they ministered. Their pastor told me to be careful with the young people. "They could be interrogated, beaten, or go to prison for traveling with you."

It was quite a culture shock to return to the United States and preach in large youth conferences. What a contrast to hear musicians brag about driving Mercedes Benzes. They sold shirts, beach towels, and anything else young people would buy with their pictures and names on them.

No wonder we don't have revival in America. We are so busy promoting ourselves that we don't have time to proclaim Jesus Christ. When revival comes, there is but one purpose in our music: the promotion of the glory of God.

A third characteristic of revival is a keen awareness that God Himself is the chief audience of our worship. In a church that has experienced awakening, many times the congregation sings without hymnbooks. This is because of a lack of literature in many communist-bloc countries, but as a result they sing only songs with which they are familiar. They don't seem so caught up with the intricacy of their music as with the simplicity of its message. They lift their heads and bellow their songs toward heaven. It becomes clear to Whom they are singing.

Music is a vehicle that transports what is on the heart of man to the throne of God. The awakened church has worship and adoration on her heart.

A fourth characteristic of worship in the revived church is that it is participation-oriented rather than performance-oriented. The first time I visited Romania, I arrived about an hour prior to a worship service. I was surprised to find that people had already begun to gather. Scattered around the auditorium were people quietly praying or reading the Scriptures. They had come to worship.

The worship service included choir singing, poetry reading, praying, congregational singing, and preaching. There were few spectators, just participators.

This has been the way of the revived church for centuries. Thus, Paul and Silas could worship in prison as well as in the sanctuary. Luther's music emphasized congregational singing. True worship is always a people's movement.

A fifth characteristic of worship in the revived church is that it has been hammered out of human experience. At the conclusion of a week of secret discipleship meetings in Romania, we had Communion with the university students we had discipled. The leader played a guitar and sang in English, "You are my Hiding Place. You always fill my heart with songs of deliverance. Whenever I am afraid, I will trust in You. I will trust in You. Let the weak say, 'I am strong in the strength of the Lord.' "

After singing in English, the students closed their eyes and sang in Romanian. Their worship was beautiful because God is their Hiding Place. Those students lived under the fear of imprisonment, but God was their security. Their music was an expression of what they had discovered.

This has been true throughout history. A biographer wrote, "Because Handel lived fully with his heart, his suffering was deep, but out of it came his great music."[4]

Other great hymn writers have written from the depths of their experience. The family of Chicago businessman H.G. Spafford went down with a French steamer. Spafford's wife was rescued, but their four children drowned. Through deep pain, he wrote a poem that has become one of the great hymns of the past century, "It Is Well with My Soul."

"When peace, like a river, attendeth my way, When

4. Ibid., p. 59.

sorrows like sea billows roll; Whatever my lot, Thou hast taught me to say, It is well, it is well with my soul."[5]

The final characteristic of worship in the revived church is that the quality of public worship is directly related to the quality of our private worship.

Revival grows out of hearts that seek God. When those hearts find God, there is a joy explosion. A new song reigns.

The fruit of the awakened church will be in her worship of the true and living God, worship in Spirit and Truth, rooted in truth that God Himself is the object of the worship.

The church in the West has produced some of the most exciting, talented, and creative Christian musicians, but we must recognize that talent and creativity do not in themselves constitute awakening. Much of contemporary Christian music is more entertainment than worship.

In the United States recently, a talented, contemporary Christian music group was singing prior to my speaking to 10,000 young people. To advertise their latest album, they threw huge beach balls out among the young people as they sang. The young people climbed over each other trying to touch the beach balls.

The arena became chaotic. The youth began doing "the Wave." Thousands lost complete sense of any worship experience. To say the least, it was difficult to preach after that.

Several months earlier I heard a very popular contemporary Christian musician say on national television that she had taught this generation of Christians that it was OK "to dance your brains out."

The purpose of Christian music is *not* entertainment. It is worship. True worship will bypass neither the intel-

5. Cited in John Loveland, comp., *Blessed Assurance—The Life and Hymns of Fanny J. Crosby* (Nashville: Broadman, 1978), p. 134.

lect nor the will. True worship involves mind, will, and emotions.

Contemporary musicians should remember the words of Handel when the *Messiah* was first performed in Dublin in 1742. A nobleman complimented the composer on the great entertainment of the *Messiah*. Handel replied, "My Lord, I should be sorry if I only entertained them. I wished to make them better."[6] And we are better people because of his music.

We could experience one of the greatest revivals of all time if we would learn to worship. We were created for that purpose.

We cannot afford for Sunday mornings to be funeral dirges. Nor can we afford to allow this generation of Christian young people to be satisfied with the passing winds of Christian entertainment. We must give ourselves to worshiping the Father.

6. *A Gift of Music*; p. 62.

12
DISCIPLESHIP—THE WINESKIN FOR AWAKENING

The lives of the Apostles, especially that of St. Paul, reveal an unusual and brilliant concept of missionary strategy. They always went first to the great cities located on the trade routes. From these centers their disciples and converts then travelled out to the towns beyond and there established churches which in turn established still others. . . .

Above all they founded congregations. The Apostles enjoined upon their converts the responsibility to become the church.[1]
—William Stuart McBirnie

My first few months at the Hahn Baptist Church in West Germany were difficult for me. I realized that we would not know how to handle an awakening if it were to come to us. I prayed, studied, and listened to find some solution. I listened to a tape of a speaker from a parachurch organization who encouraged pastors to meet with men who were hungry for God and to teach them everything they knew about walking with God.

I accepted the challenge and asked God to give me six

1. William S. McBirnie, *The Search for the Twelve Apostles* (Wheaton, Ill.: Tyndale, 1981), pp. 22–23.

men who wanted to follow Jesus more than anything else in life. Tex asked God to do the same thing with some ladies. What God did in the next few months placed within my heart a new hope for the church in the West. First, we saw lasting fruit. I look back on those years as pastor with a deep sense of satisfaction. Those people are today walking with Jesus.

I saw not only lasting fruit, but also *multiplying* fruit. Most of those men and women are not only growing in Christ, but they are also serving the Lord as lay people and vocational ministers in many congregations. The greatest joy of my ministry has been to watch those people become spiritual multipliers.

The last and great commission Jesus gave His followers before ascending to the Father was to make disciples. The objective of the church was not to build an organization, but to build an organism made up of people who had decided to follow Jesus and learn of Him. The objective became "people," to win people and grow them in Christ so that they could in turn win others. Every man and woman was to become a soul winner and a disciplemaker. Any church doing less than that has ceased to fulfill Christ's objective for His church.

If a bakery does not produce baked goods, there is something radically wrong with it. By the same token, there is something radically wrong with the church that is not winning people to Christ and helping them grow spiritually. The church must enable every member of its congregation to win souls and make disciples. God never intended for the pastor to win all the souls and teach all the classes. Revival will produce a well-mobilized laity for God's glory.

When I began to meet with the men of our church, I had no well-organized program. I had only a vision for what God intended His church to be. That was probably one of the greatest contributing factors to the discipleship that was to follow. Most of us think of discipleship as a neat packaged program, but discipleship is a way of life.

I shared a way of life with those men. I began by praying with them. Then I taught witnessing and the way of the cross. Here is what happened with several:

DON SHELTON: Don had been a Christian for several years. He had attempted to teach an adult Sunday school class, felt uncomfortable with public speaking, and did not continue. He submitted to the discipleship ministry, and he led a number of people to Christ and became a discipleship leader. Don eventually became chairman of the deacons. When he retired from the military, God called him to preach the gospel. He was later called by Hahn Baptist Church as their pastor. The church has grown tremendously under Don's preaching and teaching. Scores have come to Christ through his ministry.

ED TRACEY: Ed and his wife were having marital problems when they came to the church. They committed their lives to Jesus and submitted to discipleship. Not only did God do a marvelous work in their home, but they also began to reach others for Christ. Ed was a crew chief for the Air Force. Before I left for Europe, Ed and his crew took Tex and me out for lunch. What a thrill to hear each man give his testimony. Every one of them had given his life to Christ after Ed began to follow Christ and witness at work.

JOHN LABASH: John, a relatively new Christian when he came to Germany, was hospital administrator on the base. He was instrumental in bringing the hospital commander, Col. Spencer Downs, to Christ. Dr. Downs later became the Surgeon General of the Air National Guard. He is presently retired from the military and is attending seminary. Dr. Downs believes God has called him to a full-time vocational ministry. John continues to walk with God and make disciples.

KEN LEEBURG: The defense attorney on the base, Ken was the first man that I discipled. Ken led numerous people to Christ through his job and became a Sunday school teacher and a deacon before he was killed in an automobile accident.

JERRY ANDERSON: The first Sunday Jerry attended the church, he made a commitment of his life to Jesus. After he submitted himself to discipleship, he told me one day, "I must lead someone in my squadron to Jesus. If I leave Hahn without doing that, I will not have fulfilled God's purpose for my life here." He led several in his squadron to Jesus. Later, Jerry became a deacon and an adult Sunday school teacher. God called him to the ministry. He left the military to give his life to a full-time vocational ministry.

SCOTT BLOOM: One day while jogging I was struck by a hit-and-run driver. Scott and his wife found me lying in the field and called an ambulance. The next Sunday Scott came to church for the first time. He made a commitment of his life to Jesus and became a part of the men's discipleship group. Scott eventually became a discipleship leader and led several people to Christ. He continues to serve the Lord in the military.

Many more became involved in the discipleship ministry and became spiritual multipliers, but those few portray what discipleship can be in a local church.

True discipleship is rooted in evangelism and then blossoms into spiritual growth. Discipleship not rooted in evangelism is simply "sheep swapping." Scores of Christians travel from one church to another, and one discipleship group to another, looking for some deeper truth. These people must cease searching for more truth and begin applying the truth they already know. They must become soul winners.

As we commit ourselves to disciplemaking, we will build a "new wineskin" that will contain the "new wine" of revival. God has not sent revival to the West because we would not know what to do with it. The new believers would go out the back door as quickly as they came through the front. Discipleship is the means to close the back door.

We have ushered people into Bible studies, workbooks, and discipleship groups without the proper understanding of what it costs to be a disciple of Jesus. When Jesus called for disciples, He challenged them to count the cost. Jesus told one man that it would cost his material wealth to follow Him. He told another that he had to put Him before his father's funeral. He told others that their relationship with Him had to be greater than their most intimate family relationships. Jesus didn't make it easy. He was looking for men and women who meant business. The bottom line of discipleship was that an individual had to be "willing to lose his life." Only then could he find life in the kingdom of God.

We need men and women today who are willing to pay the price. I knew the night I became a Christian that God wanted me in the ministry. The man who led me to Christ explained to me the cost of following Jesus. "Sam, Jesus didn't have to leave heaven to die for you. He chose to. He suffered and bled and was ridiculed and tortured. He gave His life for you. If He's called you to preach, then you must be willing to give Him everything regardless of the cost. Even if it means going to jail or losing your friends, you must be willing to pay the price." I've always been thankful for his telling it to me straight. A precedent was set for my walk with Jesus.

When a person comes to Jesus in Eastern Europe, he comes with a keen understanding of the demand of discipleship. He knows it may cost his position, his education, or even his family. Perhaps the problem in the West is that we have made the decision an easy one. We need to understand the demands of discipleship.

If we are to be true disciples of Jesus, we must by grace learn the disciplines of the Christian life. Discipline is one of the most remarkable traits of the new Christians in Eastern Europe.

My family, a group of American Christians, some young Romanian believers, and I spent a week together in the mountains of Romania. The Romanian university students were mostly new Christians. The Americans were going to teach and encourage these new believers. When the week concluded, it was we Americans who had been taught and encouraged. The Romanian young people were more committed to the disciplines of the Christian life than any youth I had ever met.

The leader of these young people was memorizing the entire New Testament. We never asked him, "What verse are you trying to memorize today?" We always asked, "What book are you trying to memorize?"

We would ask these new Christians to turn to a particular passage, but their leader would say, "No." He would point to one of them. "Quote the verse." There were few verses in our Bible studies that these new believers had not already memorized.

The Scriptures are sacred to the Christians of Eastern Europe. They do not have access to Christian literature and Christian media that we have in the West. This has forced many of the young believers to become disciplined in their walk with God.

Four basic disciplines are needed in the church if we are to experience awakening. Two of these affect our relationship with God, and two affect our relationship with our fellow men.

Our life in prayer and in the Word of God will reflect our spiritual growth. We discover Jesus through the Scriptures. Jesus is proclaimed from Genesis to Revelation. We must be faithful to that time alone with God. There will be some dry times in prayer, but we must remain faithful and disciplined. I have never known anyone to reach the mountaintop without having first walked through the valley.

Our life as a witness and our fellowship in the church will reflect our relationship with people. There must be a new commitment to the local church. Faithfulness to the universal Body of Christ will be manifested in the local congregation. When revival comes, it will have its expression in local congregations.

True disciplemaking will produce disciples loyal to the local church. The purpose of discipleship is to produce men and women who are an expression of the glory of Jesus. That glory is discovered in the context of a local group. We are each unique and have grown in different ways, so it is in the context of a group that we can see fuller expression of the life and character of Christ. We need the fellowship of other Christians to experience revival.

Witnessing is the most difficult of all of the disciplines for most believers. This discipline forces us into risk and confrontation. However, it also carries the greatest reward. There is no greater joy than to lead another person to Jesus.

When we have all four disciplines functioning in our lives, then we are in a position for revival.

The disciple's destiny is simply conformity to the image of Christ. When we hunger and thirst for His righteousness, then we shall be filled.

There is a cry for revival in the land, but we must remember that true revival will result in the letting go of old habits and thought patterns. It means we must develop His pattern for every detail of our lives. We must become like Jesus.

When we are committed to that, the Holy Spirit will breathe on the church in sweet revival.

> Breath on us, oh, Holy Spirit
> Revive Your church today!
> Manifest the glory of Jesus
> And transform us by Your power.
> It is only the beauty of Your light
> That gives us hope in this hour.
> Breathe on us, oh, Holy Spirit
> Revive Your church today!